1430 W. Susquehanna Ave
Philadelphia, PA 19121
215-236-1760 | treehousebooks.org

THE FIRST BOOK
OF FESTIVALS

Published by Evans Brothers Limited in 2005
2A Portman Mansions
Chiltern St
London W1U 6NR

Ganeri, Anita
A first book of festivals
1.Fasts and feasts – Juvenile literature
I. Title
204.8

ISBN 0 237 53104 6
13-digit ISBN (from 1 January 2007)
978 0 237 53104 1

Acknowledgements
Editorial: Julia Bird
Design: Simon Borrough
Production: Jenny Mulvanny

The author and publishers would like to thank the
following for permission to reproduce photographs:
Cover: Corbis, page 18: Collections © Geoff
Howard, page 19: Helene Rogers/Art Director's &
Trip, page 24 : ArkReligion.com/Helene Rogers,
page 25: Getty Images/The Image Bank, page 30:
© Ross Ressmeyer/Corbis, page 31: CIRCA/Barrie
Searle, page 36: Topfoto, p.37: Helene Rogers/Art
Director's & Trip, p.42: CIRCA/William Holtby,
p.43: CIRCA, p.48: © Gideon Mendel/Corbis,
p.49: Peters Sanders Photography, p.52: CIRCA/
Bipin Mistry, p.53: © Asim Tanveer/ Reuters/
Corbis, p.58: ArkReligion.com/ Dinodia, p.59:
Corbis, p.64: © Jose Fuste Raga/Corbis, p.65:
Circa/William Holtby, p.70: © Blaine Harrington
III/Corbis, p.71: Desai Noshir/Corbis Sygma

THE FIRST BOOK OF FESTIVALS

Anita Ganeri

With activities by Mary Saunders

Introduction

Festivals are a vital and vibrant part of every religious tradition. They are times of both celebration and remembrance, when members of a faith mark special occasions within their religion. Many religious festivals have their origins in ancient times and began as ways of marking key times of the year, such as the coming of spring or the gathering in of the harvest. Other festivals may commemorate important events in a religion's history or in the lives of a religion's founders, teachers and deities.

Some religious festivals are marked only locally. Others are celebrated all over the world. Celebrations vary according to the culture of a particular country, although the significance of the key festivals remains the same everywhere. To mark out a festival as a special occasion, people celebrate with prayers, services, feasts and special items of food, decorations, gifts, cards, processions, music and dance. Crucially, festivals also provide members of a religion with the opportunity to worship and practise their faith together, to share special occasions with their friends, families and communities, and to show their commitment to their faith.

For children, learning about festivals is a fascinating and accessible way of finding out about a religion's beliefs. The comparison can be made between the role of festivals in people's religious lives and special times in a child's life, such as birthdays. How and why are these celebrated? How does this makes the children feel? It is important to stress, however, that festivals are not simply times of celebration for members of different faiths but have a deeper meaning. A good starting point for explaining and exploring this meaning is the story behind most of the festivals.

About this book

This book covers key festivals in the six main world faiths - Christianity, Judaism, Islam, Hinduism, Buddhism and Sikhism. It begins with a brief introduction to each of these faiths and some background notes to the festivals, to place them within their religious context. Simple retellings of the stories behind the festivals follow, which are suitable for reading out loud to the class. Each story is prefaced by two large-format photographs illustrating aspects of how the festival is celebrated. Each festival is backed up by a range of activities, with ideas for extension projects, support and early learning goals. Finally, there is a festival calendar for each of the faiths and a glossary of unfamiliar terms.

Health and Safety

Some of the activities in this book involve food and cooking. Nursery practitioners and teachers should be aware of any special dietary requirements or allergies that affect the children in their care, and should of course also follow basic safety and hygiene procedures.

Contents

Christianity

Christianity is based on the teachings of Jesus Christ, a preacher and healer, who lived in the 1st century BCE in Palestine. Christians believe that Jesus was the Son of God who came to Earth to save people from sin. After Jesus's death, his many followers became missionaries, spreading his teachings far and wide. Today, Christianity is the world's largest religion, with some 2,000 million followers.

The life of Jesus

According to the Bible, Jesus was born in Bethlehem, where his mother, Mary, and earthly father, Joseph, had been summoned by the Roman governor to take part in a census. Because the town was crowded and every inn was full, Jesus was born in a humble stable.

We know little about Jesus's youth. Palestine was a mainly Jewish country and Jesus was brought up as a Jew. He lived in Nazareth and probably followed in his father's footsteps and worked as a carpenter.

When Jesus was about 30, he was baptised by his cousin, John. This marked the beginning of a new life in which Jesus travelled all over Palestine, teaching people about God. Ordinary people flocked to hear him, but the Jewish leaders believed their authority threatened by his growing popularity. They had Jesus arrested, charged with blasphemy and sentenced to death by crucifixion. Christians believe that, three days after he died on the cross, Jesus was resurrected, or rose from the dead.

Christian beliefs

Christians believe in one God who created the world and watches over it. They compare him to a loving father. God is all-powerful, everlasting and omnipresent. Three aspects of God are referred to – God the Father, God the Son, and God the Holy Spirit. These are called the Holy Trinity.

Christians believe that Jesus was the Son of God, that is, God in human form. He was sent to Earth and gave up his own life in order to save people from sin. For Christians, his Resurrection shows that if they follow him and lead good lives, they too can achieve everlasting life with God. Jesus became known as the Christ, which means 'anointed one' or Messiah.

Christians worship God in different ways. Many worship at home, in private. Many attend services in church, particularly on Sunday, the day of rest and prayer. Services include hymns, prayers and Bible readings, and are usually led by a priest or minister. For most Christians, the most important part of a service is a ceremony called the Eucharist, Mass or Holy Communion. Worshippers share bread and wine blessed by the minister or priest, in remembrance of the Last Supper.

The Bible

The Christians' holy book is the Bible, a collection of 66 books, divided into the Old and New Testaments. The Old Testament contains books of history, poetry and law, and tells how God created the world and of God's relationship with his chosen people, the Israelites. It is largely the same as the Tenakh, the ancient Jewish scriptures. The New Testament includes the four Gospels (Matthew, Mark, Luke and John) which give accounts of Jesus's life and teaching. It also contains writings by the early Christians and accounts of the establishment of the early Christian Church.

For Christians, the Bible is a very special book which forms the basis of their beliefs. They believe that it reveals God's will and use it as a guide for how to live their lives.

Christian Festivals

Christmas

At Christmas, Christians celebrate the birth of Jesus Christ. Christmas Day falls on 25 December, although no one knows exactly when Jesus was born. This date was chosen by the early Christians some 300 years after Jesus's birth. It was also the date of an ancient Roman winter festival, anticipating the coming of spring after the long winter. (In the Orthodox Church, Christmas Day falls on 7 January because the Church uses a different calendar.) For Christians, Christmas marks the coming of God to Earth in the form of Jesus, the greatest gift God could give to the world and a cause for great rejoicing.

Religious celebrations include church services, such as Midnight Mass on Christmas Eve and a service on Christmas morning. People sing carols, say prayers thanking God, and listen to readings from the Bible (the story of Jesus's birth is found in the Bible, in the Gospels of St Luke and St Matthew. It is retold on pages 20-21.) Most churches have a crib, a model of the stable in which Jesus was born with figures of Mary, Joseph, Jesus and animals, such as an ox and an ass.

But Christmas is a time of celebration for Christians and non-Christians alike. The custom of present-giving reminds Christians of the wise men's visit to Jesus and the gifts they brought, but it may have its origins in the Roman winter festival. There are many stories about who delivers Christmas gifts, including, of course, that of St Nicholas (Santa Claus). Legend says that he was a bishop who lived many years ago in Turkey, a far cry from his current home at the North Pole! He was said to be kind-hearted, especially to the poor.

Easter

Although Christmas is more widely celebrated, Easter is the most important festival in the Christian year. Easter falls in March or April and is the time when Christians remember the last week of Jesus's life, called Holy Week. It begins with Palm Sunday, when Jesus rode into Jerusalem on a donkey to celebrate the Jewish festival of Pesach (Passover). People greeted him as their king and saviour and threw palm fronds in his path. This custom continues today when church-goers receive palm-leaf crosses. On Thursday, Jesus ate a final meal, the Last Supper, with his disciples. At this meal, Jesus shared bread and wine with them and commanded them to do this in future to remember him. This Thursday is called Maundy Thursday, from the Latin word 'mandatum', meaning 'a command'.

Friday (Good Friday) of Holy Week commemorates the crucifixion of Jesus. On this solemn day, churches are cleared of decorations and flowers, and left dark and plain. Many churches hold a service of silent prayer and meditation between noon and three o'clock, representing the time that Jesus is believed to have hung from the cross. Hot cross buns are traditionally eaten on this day. No special ceremonies take place on Holy Saturday, but Easter Sunday is a joyful day on which Jesus is believed to have risen from the dead. Churches are decked with flowers and church bells rung. Many Easter symbols, such as Easter eggs and rabbits, are reminders of new life. They signify Jesus's Resurrection but have their origins in ancient spring festivals when new life in nature was celebrated. (The story of Easter is retold on pages 26-27.)

Judaism

Judaism is the religion of the Jews. According to Jewish law, anyone with a Jewish mother is a Jew, whether they practise their religion or not. With its origins in the Middle East over 4,000 years ago, Judaism is one of the world's oldest faiths. Today, there are some 15 million Jews, living all over the world. The largest Jewish communities are concentrated in Israel, the USA and Europe.

Jewish history

According to the Jewish scriptures, the first Jew was Abraham, the leader of a nomadic tribe called the Hebrews. He became known as the father of the Jewish people. Abraham taught people to worship one God, rather than many different gods, as was the custom at the time. Jews believe that God made a covenant (agreement) with Abraham. If Abraham and his descendants worshipped God, God would look after them and give them their own land to live in. This was the Promised Land of Canaan (modern-day Israel).

Although the Jews settled in Canaan, famine forced their descendants to move to Egypt in search of food. There, they were forced to work as slaves and suffered terribly. God chose Moses to lead the Jews out of Egypt. This was called the Exodus. After many years of wandering in the desert, the Jews finally reached their Promised Land.

Jewish scriptures

The Jewish scriptures are called the Tenakh. The Tenakh consists of three parts – the Torah (five books of teaching), the Nevi'im (21 books of the prophets) and the Ketuvim (13 books of writings). The name Tenakh comes from the initials of the three parts – T, N and K.

For Jews, the Torah is the most important part of the scriptures. They believe that God gave the Torah to Moses on Mount Sinai, as the Jews wandered through the desert after the Exodus from Egypt. It contains teachings and rules for Jews to live their lives by, summed up by the Ten Commandments, or Ten Sayings. Copies of the Torah are treated with great care and respect. They are handwritten on scrolls and kept in the synagogue, in a special alcove called the Holy Ark. This is the holiest part of the synagogue which people face as they pray.

Jewish life and worship

Jews can worship in private anywhere. Traditionally, there are three main prayer times – morning, afternoon and evening. Many Jews choose to attend the synagogue to pray with others. Synagogues are not solely places of worship, however, but places where the whole community can meet, study and celebrate.

Many synagogues have daily services but the services held on the Shabbat (Sabbath) are the most important. The Shabbat morning service includes readings from the Torah, prayers and blessings. It is led by a rabbi. At synagogue services, men wear a small cap, called a kippah, to show respect for God. Traditional Jews may also wear a prayer 'shawl' and two small leather boxes, called tefillin, which contain passages from the scriptures.

Shabbat lasts from dusk on Friday night until Saturday evening. It is a day of rest and prayer which reminds Jews of how God created the world in six days, then rested on the seventh. Marking Shabbat at home is a very important part of Jewish life. Shabbat begins with the lighting of the Shabbat candles on Friday night, followed by a family meal. On Saturday night, a 'farewell' ceremony marks the end of Shabbat.

Jewish Festivals

Pesach

One of the most important times in the Jewish year, Pesach falls in March or April. Along with Sukkot and Shavuot, it is one of the three 'pilgrim' festivals, so called because it was once the custom for Jews to make a pilgrimage to Jerusalem at these times, to visit the Temple, their holiest building. At Pesach, Jews remember the Exodus from Egypt, when God helped their ancestors to escape from slavery in Egypt and led them to safety in the Promised Land of Canaan (modern-day Israel). (This story is retold on pages 32-33.)

The time before Pesach is extremely busy in a Jewish household. The whole house is cleaned from top to bottom (Pesach is also a spring festival and a time of new beginnings) and every trace of food made with yeast is removed. This is a reminder of how, in their hurry to escape from Egypt, the Jews did not wait for their bread dough to rise but baked flat loaves (matzot) instead. But the focus of Pesach is the Pesach supper, called the Seder, eaten on the first night of the festival. In Hebrew, seder means 'order' and refers to the fact that every part of the supper happens in a set order, to mark the transition from slavery to freedom. The meal begins with the youngest person at the table asking four traditional questions about the past. The questions and answers are read from the Haggadah, a book which tells the story of Pesach. As the story is read, people taste the foods on the Seder plate. As with the matzot, each of these all symbolise an aspect of the Jews' life in Egypt (see picture captions and activities pages).

Hanukkah

Hanukkah, the Jewish festival of lights, is celebrated in November or December. The festival lasts for eight days and remembers an episode from Jewish history when some Jews, known as the Maccabees, won back the Temple of Jerusalem from their Syrian Greek enemies. When the Maccabees tried to relight the Temple lamp, they found only enough oil to last for one day. Then a miracle happened and God kept the lamp burning brightly for eight days until fresh supplies arrived. (This story is retold on pages 38-39.) For most Jews, this miracle had a deeper meaning. The light that is the Jewish faith seemed to be in peril but it could not be put out. It also showed how important it was for the Jews to stand up for what they believed in, even when their lives were in danger.

The central part of Hanukkah celebrations is the lighting of candles on the hanukiah, a nine-branched candlestick. Eight of the candles stand for the eight nights of Hanukkah; the ninth is used to light the other candles. On the first night, one candle is lit; on the second night, two, and so on until the last night when all eight candles are burning. Afterwards, prayers are said and the hanukiah is displayed on a windowsill to proclaim the miracle. Traditionally, food fried in oil is eaten at Hanukkah as a reminder of the oil in the Temple lamp (see page 39). People also play games, such as dreidel (see pages 40-41). The Hebrew letters written on the four sides of the dreidel are the initials of the words which spell out the phrase which says 'A great miracle happened there'.

Islam

Islam is the religion followed by the Muslims and means 'obedience' or 'submission'. Muslims obey or submit to the will of Allah (God) and try to live in the way that Allah wishes them to. Islam began in the Middle East about 1,400 years ago. Today, it has some 1,000 million followers spread all over the world and is the world's fastest growing religion.

The life of Muhammad

Muslims believe that Islam began with Adam, the first in a line of prophets chosen by Allah to teach people how to live. They believe that their religion was 'completed' by the last and greatest of these prophets, Muhammad.

Muhammad was born in Makkah, Arabia (modern Saudi Arabia) in about 570 CE. Orphaned at an early age, he was brought up by his grandfather, then by his uncle. Although Muhammad became successful and prosperous, he was dismayed by the greed and corruption he saw around him. He spent long periods alone, meditating and praying, in the hills outside Makkah.

One night, as Muhammad was meditating in a cave on Mount Hira, the angel, Jibril, appeared and began to reveal Allah's message. Many more revelations followed throughout Muhammad's life. These were later collected together and written down as the Qur'an, the Muslim holy book. After the first revelation, Muhammad returned to Makkah and began to teach people about Allah. Many people came to hear him but some Makkan merchants felt threatened by his message and plotted to kill him. In 622 CE, Muhammad fled to Madinah where he established the first Muslim community. He died in Madinah in 632 CE.

Muslim beliefs and worship

The key beliefs of Islam are summed up in five practices, called the Five Pillars of Islam, because they support the faith of Islam, just as real pillars support a building. These are:

1. Shahadah, or statement of faith. It says, "There is no God but Allah and Muhammad is the Prophet of Allah". It sums up the Muslim belief that Allah is the one true God who created the world and everything in it. Allah is all-powerful, all-seeing and all-knowing. The Qur'an gives 99 names which describe aspects of Allah's power, for example the Merciful, the Generous, the Forgiver and the Kind.

2. Salah, or prayer. Muslims pray five times a day – at dawn, midday, mid-afternoon, in the evening and at night. Muslims must face Makkah as they pray but can pray anywhere, as long as it is clean. As they say their prayers in Arabic, they go through a series of prayer positions. Some Muslims go to the mosque to say their daily prayers. All Muslims try to go to the mosque for midday prayers on Fridays.

3. Zakah, or giving money to the poor. All Muslims who can afford it are expected to make an annual donation as zakah. This reminds them of Allah's generosity and helps those less well off than themselves.

4. Sawm, or fasting. Muslims must fast during daylight hours during the holy month of Ramadan. Fasting is believed to teach people self-discipline and a greater understanding of those less fortunate than themselves. The end of Ramadan is marked by the festival of Id-ul-Fitr.

5. Hajj, or pilgrimage. This means making a pilgrimage to the holy city of Makkah, birthplace of the Prophet Muhammad, and the most sacred site in Islam. Muslims must try to make Hajj at least once in their lifetimes.

Muslim Festivals

For Muslims, the two most important festivals are Id-ul-Adha, the Festival of the Sacrifice at the end of the Hajj pilgrimage, and Id-ul-Fitr, the Festival of the Breaking of the Fast after the holy month of Ramadan (see below for more details). Both are called 'Id', an Arabic word meaning 'feast' or 'celebration' and are times for the community to come together, not only to celebrate but to patch up quarrels and help those who are poor, lonely or needy. There are many similiarities in the ways in which the two festivals are celebrated. Both begin with people dressing in their best clothes and attending communal prayers in the mosque. Many people exchange cards and gifts of sweets, and children go to Id parties.

Id-ul-Adha

Id-ul-Adha is known as 'Greater Id' because it is a more important religious festival than Id-ul-Fitr. It lasts for four days in the Muslim month of Dhul-Hijjah at the end of the Hajj pilgrimage to Makkah. At Id-ul-Adha, Muslims remember the story of the Prophet Ibrahim (Abraham) and his willingness to sacrifice his beloved son, Isma'il, in order to show his devotion to Allah. As Ibrahim is ready to kill Isma'il, Allah intervenes to spare him and a ram is sacrificed instead. The story is told in the Qur'an (this story is retold on pages 44-45). To commemorate this event, Muslims who can afford to do so sacrifice an animal, such as a sheep, goat or camel. Some of the meat is shared out among friends and family. Some is given to the poor so that they

too can join in with the Id festivities. The sacrifice symbolises people's willingness to obey Allah at whatever cost to themselves.

The Hajj is one of the Five Pillars of Islam (see left). All Muslims who are able try to make the pilgrimage to Makkah at least once in their lifetimes. Muslims taking part in the Hajj also observe various ceremonies which remember the story of Ibrahim and Isma'il. At a place called Mina, they throw stones at three pillars which represent the sites where the Devil tried to tempt Isma'il to disobey his father as he was leading him to the place of sacrifice.

Id-ul-Fitr

Id-ul-Fitr or 'Little Id' lasts for three days at the end of Ramadan. It begins when the new moon is sighted in the night sky. Ramadan is the Muslim holy month of fasting, when Muslims go without food and drink from daybreak to sunset. This fasting is called sawm and is one of the Five Pillars of Islam (see left). At the end of each day of Ramadan, they break their fast with some dates and water, following the example set by the Prophet Muhammad. After prayers in the mosque, they return home for their evening meal. At Id-ul-Fitr, special food is eaten, although this can vary from country to country. Unlike the other festivals in this book, Id-ul-Fitr does not have a story attached to it. Rather, it is a time when Muslims thank Allah for sending the Qu'ran to them and for giving them the strength to complete their fast at Ramadan.

Hinduism

Hinduism is the world's oldest religion. Although it has no fixed date of origin, its roots stretch back some 4,500 years to the time of the Indus Valley Civilisation in north-west India (modern Pakistan). The religious ideas of the Indus people mixed with those of later invaders to form the basis of Hinduism. Today, there are more than 800 million Hindus. Most live in India, but there are large Hindu communities in Europe, North America, South Africa and South East Asia.

Hindu beliefs

Hindus describe their religion as sanatana dharma, which means 'eternal law' or 'eternal teaching'. For Hindus, this is a code of duty and behaviour which affects every aspect of their daily lives.

Hinduism is an extremely varied religion with many different way of practising. Most Hindus, however, share the same basic beliefs. They believe in a great soul, or spirit, called Brahman, which some Hindus call God. Brahman has no visible shape or form but is present everywhere and in everything. There are also thousands of Hindu gods and goddesses, each of which represents a different aspect of Brahman's power. The three most important are Brahma, the creator of the universe, Vishnu, the protector, and Shiva, the destroyer. Vishnu and Shiva are worshipped all over India and have many mandirs dedicated to them. Two of the most popular Hindu gods are Krishna and Rama, earthly incarnations of Lord Vishnu. Both are well loved and worshipped all over India. Hindus do not worship all the deities. Some choose a particular god or goddess who has traditional links to their family, home or occupation or whom they believe has helped them in some way. Other Hindus do not worship any deities at all.

Hindus believe that every individual has a soul, called atman. When you die, your soul lives on and is reincarnated, or reborn, in another body. This happens repeatedly, trapping the soul in a cycle of birth, death and rebirth. The aim of a Hindu's life is to break free of this cycle and attain moksha, or salvation, when the individual soul, atman, merges with the great soul, Brahman. The nature of each rebirth is governed by the law of karma. Each good action takes a person closer to moksha. Each bad action leads them further away.

Hindu worship

Many Hindus visit a mandir to worship. Each mandir is dedicated to a particular deity and is believed to be the deity's home on Earth. The deity's presence is represented by a murti, or sacred image, which stands in the innermost shrine, which is the holiest part of the mandir.

The Hindu act of worship is called puja. Hindus visit the mandir for darshana, or 'viewing', of the deity. Worshippers take offerings of sweets, fruit, flowers and money, which they give to the priest. He presents them to the deity to be blessed, then gives part of the offerings back to the worshippers to bestow the deity's blessing on them. The priest also places a red mark of blessing, called a tilak, on the worshippers' foreheads.

Hindus also worship at home. Most have a shrine where they perform puja every morning and evening. The shrine may be a room, or part of room, or even a simple shelf, with a picture of the deity.

Hindu Festivals

Divali

Of all of the thousands of Hindu festivals celebrated throughout the year, Divali and Holi (see right) are the most important. They are celebrated by Hindus all over India and wherever else they have settled in the world. There are many reasons why Divali is celebrated. Many Hindus remember the ancient story of Rama and Sita, told in the Ramayana, one of the most sacred Hindu texts (this story is retold on pages 54-55). Exiled to the forest, Sita is kidnapped by the demon-king, Ravana, and taken to his palace on the island of Lanka. The story tells how Rama, helped by the monkey-god, Hanuman, rescues Sita and how they return home to be crowned king and queen. But Divali is also a time when Hindus, especially those from business communities, worship Lakshmi, the goddess of wealth and good fortune. In addition, according to one ancient Hindu calendar, Divali is the start of the new year.

In India, Divali is traditionally celebrated over five days in October or November, each with its own customs and ceremonies. In other countries, such as Britain, celebrations usually take place over the nearest weekend. Divali is a very joyful, popular festival. People exchange cards and gifts of sweets, jewellery and new clothes. They also visit the mandir for Divali puja or perform puja at home. Divali is the festival of lights (the name Divali or Deepavali means 'rows of lights'.) As part of the celebrations, people decorate their homes and mandirs with divas, small clay lamps filled with oil. The divas are intended to guide Rama and Sita safely home, and to welcome Lakshmi.

Holi

The other great festival in the Hindu year is Holi, which celebrates the coming of spring in February or March and begins with the sighting of the full moon. Traditionally, this was when farmers in northern India brought in the first wheat harvest of the year. Many legends are associated with Holi. The most commonly told story is that of a prince called Prahlad and his aunt, the wicked witch, Holika (this story is retold on pages 60-61). The festival also has connections with the god, Krishna.

The length of the festival varies, but it usually lasts for at least two or three days in India; in Britain, celebrations take place over one day only, often at the weekend. Holi customs vary greatly from place to place, but many have clear links with the stories above. On the first night of Holi, people light bonfires as reminders of the story of Holika and to signify how good triumphs over evil. They gather round the fire, and throw coconuts and rice into the flames as offerings to the gods. Another popular custom is to spray each other with coloured paints and powder. This reminds people of the story of how mischief-loving Krishna once drenched his friends, the gopis (milkmaids), with coloured water. A range of objects are used as sprayers, from water pistols to bicycle pumps. Everyone is expected to join in the fun!

Buddhism

Buddhism began about 2,500 years ago in India. It is based on the teachings of an Indian prince, Siddhartha Gautama, who dedicated his life to finding a way to overcome the suffering he saw around him. He became the Buddha, which means enlightened one. Today, there are about 400 million Buddhists, mostly living in Asia. Recently, Buddhism has also attracted many followers in Europe and North America.

The life of the Buddha

Siddhartha Gautama was born in north-east India (modern Nepal) in about 563 BCE, the son of a local king. At Siddhartha's birth, a wise man told the king that his son would be either a great ruler or a great sage, depending on what he saw of life. Determined that his son should inherit his throne, the king attempted to shield Siddhartha from the trials and tribulations of the outside world. Despite growing up in great luxury, however, Siddhartha felt there was something missing from his life.

At the age of 29, without his father's knowledge, Siddhartha rode his chariot outside the palace. He saw a sick man, an old man, and a dead man – the first suffering he had ever seen. Then he saw an itinerant holy man who, despite having nothing, seemed happy and content. This experience changed Siddhartha's life. He vowed to follow the holy man's example and that night left the palace to find an answer to the problem of suffering.

For many years, Siddhartha tried to find the answer by leading a very strict life, but this did not produce the answers he sought. Eventually, he came to the village of Bodh Gaya in northern India and sat under a tree to meditate. There, he gained enlightenment and became the Buddha. The Buddha spent the rest of his life as a wandering monk, travelling around India with his followers, teaching. He died in the town of Kushinagara, aged 80.

Buddhist beliefs

Buddhist beliefs are based on the dharma, the name given to the Buddha's teachings. Dharma is one of the Three Jewels of Buddhism, together with the Buddha himself and the sangha, or community of Buddhist monks, nuns and lay people.

Two key parts of the Buddha's teaching are the Four Noble Truths and the Noble Eightfold Path. The Four Noble Truths teach that people suffer because they are never content with what they have. But suffering can be overcome by following the Noble Eightfold Path. This is a way of living and thinking that is a middle way between great luxury and great hardship. It shows eight ways for people to live: right understanding; right thought; right speech; right action; right livelihood; right effort; right mindfulness and right concentration. Buddhists believe that this path will eventually lead to nirvana, a state of perfect peace where suffering ceases.

Importantly, Buddhists do not worship the Buddha as a god. Rather they honour him as an exceptional human being. They show their respect for the Buddha by placing offerings of candles, incense and flowers in front of an image of the Buddha in a vihara (temple or monastery) or at a shrine at home. They also recite their commitment to the Three Jewels. Some Buddhists follow the Buddha's example by becoming monks or nuns.

Buddhist Festivals

There are many Buddhist festivals throughout the year, marking important times in the Buddha's life or from Buddhist history. They are greatly influenced by the culture of the various countries in which Buddhism has become established. Many festivals are specific to different groups of Buddhists - the two main schools of Buddhism are Theravada ('the way of the elders'), mainly practised in Sri Lanka, Myanmar (Burma), Thailand, Cambodia and Laos; and Mahayana ('the great vehicle'), practised in various forms in Nepal, China, Japan, Korea, Vietnam and Tibet. Because Buddhism has spread so widely, ways of celebrating festivals have mixed and mingled with local traditions and customs. Most Buddhist festivals fall at the time of the full moon, which is when the key events in the Buddha's life are believed to have occurred.

Wesak

The festival of Wesak falls at the time of the full moon in April or May. For Theravada Buddhists everywhere, this is the most important festival of the year when they commemorate the birth, enlightenment and death of the Buddha (the story is retold on pages 66-67). These three events are supposed to have occurred on the same day of the year (Mahayana Buddhists celebrate them separately on different days). The emphasis of Wesak is on the Buddha's enlightenment. At Wesak, Buddhists decorate their homes and viharas with lights as symbols of the Buddha's enlightenment. These lights light up the darkness in the same way that the Buddha's teachings light up the world and dispel ignorance. Recently, exchanging cards has become a popular part of Wesak celebrations. People also visit the vihara for a special Wesak puja and to take gifts for the monks and nuns. They may also take offerings of flowers, candles and incense to place before the image of the Buddha. Each of these is symbolic - lights stand for the Buddha's enlightenment (see above); flowers symbolise the teaching that nothing lasts for ever; the sweet smell of incense spread everywhere, like the Buddha's teaching.

In some viharas, the monks put on a special Wesak programme for children. Among other events, the children listen to stories, called Jatakas, about the Buddha's past lives. In these, the Buddha often appears as an animal to teach a particular lesson, making it easier to understand. A key Buddhist teaching is the belief in reincarnation - when you die, you are reborn in another body, human, animal or plant. So life is like a wheel, endlessly turning in a cycle of birth, death and rebirth. What keeps the wheel turning is karma - your actions and their consequences. The quality of your next life depends on how well or badly you behave in this one. The only way to stop the wheel turning and escape from the cycle is to move towards enlightenment and nirvana.

Sikhism

Sikhism originated in the 16th century in Punjab, north-west India. At that time, the two major religions of India were Hinduism and Islam. Great tension existed between the two faiths. This led a man called Nanak, a Hindu by birth, to introduce a new religion, based on tolerance and equality. Today, there are about 20 million Sikhs. Most live in India, although there are also important Sikh communities in Europe and North America.

Ten Gurus

The first of ten Sikh Gurus, or teachers, Guru Nanak was born in 1469 in a village in north-west India (modern Pakistan). When he was about 30 years old, he suddenly disappeared for a few days. When he returned to his village, he told his family that he had had a revelation from God, telling him to go out and teach people how to live good, honest lives. After this, Nanak became a wandering teacher, making long journeys to spread his message.

Guru Nanak was followed by nine other Sikh Gurus, each of whom continued to spread Nanak's teachings and establish the Sikh faith. The fifth Guru, Guru Arjan Dev, built the Harimandir, or Golden Temple, the Sikhs' holiest shrine, in the city of Amritsar.

The early Sikhs were persecuted by the Muslim rulers of India and had to fight hard for their beliefs. The ninth Guru, Guru Tegh Bahadur, was put to death for refusing to convert to Islam. The tenth Guru, Guru Gobind Singh, died in 1708. He did not name a human Guru to succeed him, but told the Sikhs that the Guru Granth Sahib, their holy book, would now be their Guru instead.

The Guru Granth Sahib

The Guru Granth Sahib is a collection of hymns and poetry 1,430 pages long. It was written by Guru Nanak, together with several of the other Gurus, with contributions by Hindu and Muslim holy men. The Guru Granth Sahib is written in Gurmukhi, the script developed by Guru Angad Dev for writing Punjabi, the language used by the Sikhs. The word Gurmukhi means 'from the Guru's mouth'.

Sikhs honour the Guru Granth Sahib as a living Guru. They believe that it is the word of God and treat it with great reverence and respect. In the Gurdwara (the Sikh place of worship), the Guru Granth Sahib is placed on a throne in the worship room, facing the congregation. A devout Sikh, called a granthi, is chosen to read from it. When not in use, the book is wrapped in a silk cloth and placed in a separate room.

Sikh beliefs and worship

Guru Nanak taught that there is one true God. Sikhs hope to grow closer to God by remembering God in everything they do, working hard and helping others. Two key Sikh beliefs are service, or sewa, and equality. Sewa means caring for others and sharing what you have. Equality means that everyone is equal in God's eyes, male or female, rich or poor, or a follower of another religion.

Sikhs visit a Gurdwara to meet and worship. The word Gurdwara means 'gateway to the Guru'. Any place that has a copy of the Guru Granth Sahib installed in it can be a Gurdwara. On entering the Gurdwara, Sikhs take off their shoes and cover their heads as a mark of respect. They bow and make offerings to the Guru Granth Sahib. A service consists of prayers, songs and readings from the Guru Granth Sahib. Afterwards, everyone shares a communal meal, called langar, to stress the belief in equality.

Sikh Festivals

Baisakhi

The Sikh festival of Baisakhi is celebrated on 13 or 14 April. It commemorates a very important event in Sikh history - the founding of the Khalsa, or Sikh community, by the tenth Guru, Guru Gobind Singh in 1699. In India, Baisakhi is also a harvest festival, marking the start of the new year when the winter wheat crop is harvested.

Baisakhi is celebrated by Sikhs across the world. Many of the customs associated with it echo the story of the founding of the Khalsa (the story is retold on pages 72-73). It is a time when many young Sikhs choose to join the Khalsa at a special amrit ceremony. The ceremony is led by five people who represent the Panj Piare (Five Beloved Ones), the first members of the Khalsa. During the ceremony, the new members sip amrit and it is also sprinkled on their hair and faces. They promise to follow the teachings of the Gurus and wear five symbols of Sikhism - kesh (uncut hair); kangha (a small, wooden comb); kara (a steel bracelet); kirpan (a small ceremonial sword) and kachera (shorts). Known as the Five Ks, each of these items has a special significance. They are also given new names - Singh (or lion) for men, and Kaur (or princess) for women - to show that they are all now members of the same family.

Traditionally, at Baisakhi, the Sikh flag, or Nishan Sahib, which flies outside the Gurdwara, is taken down, washed and cleaned. There are also services in the Gurdwara and an Akhand Path is held. This is a continuous reading of the Guru Granth Sahib, the Sikhs' holy book, from beginning to end. It is a key part of Sikh festivals. Readers work in teams, reading for about two hours at a time, and the whole reading takes about 48 hours. There are reserve readers in case anyone falls ill. In some places, there are also processions through the streets, led by people dressed as the Panj Piare.

Other Sikh festivals

The other most important festivals in the Sikh year are called gurpurbs, or 'Gurus' days. These festivals remember key events in the lives of the ten Sikh Gurus, such as their birthdays and deaths. In October or November, Sikh celebrate the birthday of the Guru Nanak, the first Sikh Guru and the founder of the Sikh faith. Like most gurpurbs, this day is marked with an Akhand Path (see above) in the Gurdwara. This is followed by the singing of shabads, together with talks to remember the significance of the day.

Christianity: Christmas

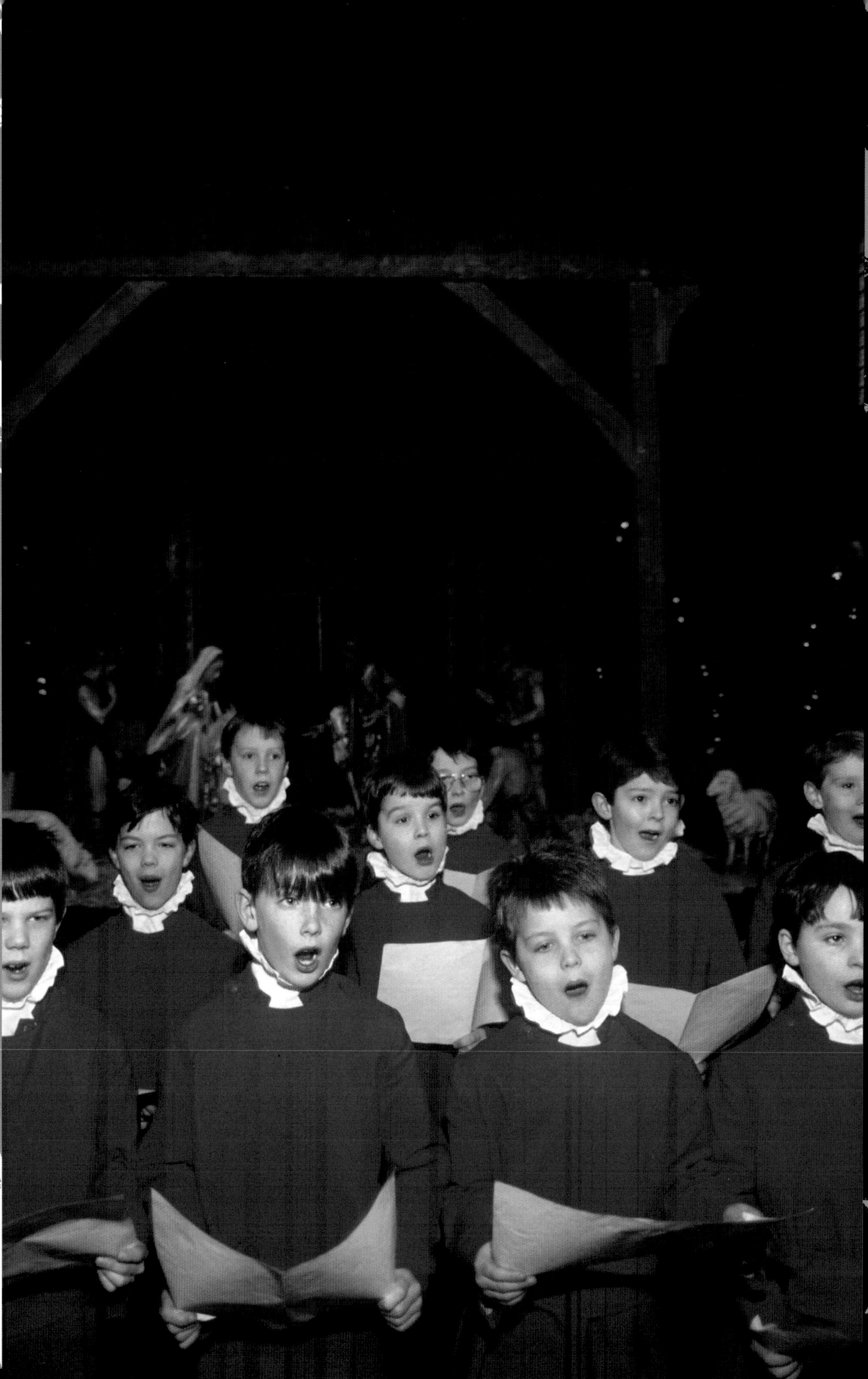

The Story of Christmas

A young woman, called Mary, lived in the town of Nazareth. One day, Mary was helping her mother with the daily chores. It was a lovely, sunny day and Mary sang as she swept the floor. Then an amazing thing happened. Suddenly, the room was filled with a bright light and a shining figure stood before her. Mary was very frightened. She dropped her broom in shock.

The figure was the angel Gabriel. He had come to deliver a special message from God.

"Don't be afraid, Mary," the angel said. "This is a happy day. God has chosen you to have a baby. You will call him Jesus and he will be a special king."

"I will do as God wishes," Mary said.

Then, in a flash, the angel was gone, just as quickly as he had appeared.

Soon afterwards, Mary married Joseph. He was a good man who worked as a carpenter. They settled down in Nazareth. But their happy life did not last for long. A little while later, the emperor sent out an order. Everyone had to go to the town where they had been born to be counted and pay their taxes. Mary and Joseph had to go to Bethlehem, a town far away where Joseph had been born. They packed up their belongings and set off.

It was a long and tiring journey. Mary rode on a donkey while Joseph walked by her side. But the road was rough and rocky, and Mary was very uncomfortable. At night, they had to sleep by the side of the road.

"Don't worry, Mary," Joseph said. "We'll soon be in Bethlehem. Then you will be able to have a good rest."

But Bethlehem was crowded with travellers, just like them. Joseph was worried. He knew that it was time for Mary's baby to be born.

So he went from door to door, looking for somewhere to stay. But all the inns were full and there were no rooms anywhere. What were they going to do?

Tired and dusty, Joseph knocked on yet another door.

"Do you have a room?" he asked the friendly innkeeper.

"I don't have a room," the innkeeper said kindly. "But you can sleep in my stable, if you like. It's not much but it's warm and clean."

Later that night, in the snug little stable, Mary had her baby boy. She called him Jesus, as the angel had said. Mary did not have a cradle for the baby. So she wrapped him in a warm blanket and laid him in a manger on some soft hay. The manger was where food was usually put for the animals. But there was nowhere else for Jesus to sleep.

On a nearby hillside, some shepherds were looking after their sheep. It was late at night and the shepherds were tired. Some of them were dozing off to sleep. Suddenly, a brilliant light filled the sky. It woke the shepherds up with a start. An angel stood in front of them. They could hardly believe their eyes.

"I have great news for you," the angel told them. "Today a very special baby has been born in Bethlehem. You will find him asleep in a stable."

As the shepherds watched, the sky filled with light. Shining angels, bright as stars, began to sing and praise God:

"Glory to God in the highest.
And on Earth peace.
Good will to all people."

When the angels had gone, the shepherds hurried to Bethlehem as fast as they could. They wanted to see the baby and worship him. They took a tiny lamb as a present. There in the stable, they found Jesus with Mary and Joseph. The shepherds knelt quietly by the manger, careful not to wake the sleeping baby. They gave the lamb to Mary, then they went back to their fields. On the way, they told everyone they met about the amazing things they had seen.

★

Far away, in the East, three wise men saw a bright new star in the sky. This was a sign that a king had been born. So they followed the star to Jerusalem to find the baby and worship him. But King Herod, the ruler of Jerusalem, was furious when he heard their news. He thought that the new king would take away his power.

"When you find this baby," he told the wise men, "come back at once and tell me. I want to worship him, too."

But wicked King Herod did not want to worship Jesus. He wanted to kill him.

The three wise men left Jerusalem and continued their journey across the desert. They rested by day and travelled by night so that they could follow the star. After many days and nights, the star led them to Bethlehem. It shone brightly above the stable where the baby Jesus lay. Joyfully, the wise men bowed down and worshipped Jesus. They also gave him precious gifts of gold, frankincense and myrrh.

Later that night, all the wise men had the same dream. An angel warned them not to go back to King Herod in Jerusalem. So the wise men went home a different way. They did not want King Herod to find the baby.

★

That same night, Joseph also saw an angel in his dreams.

"Take Mary and Jesus and go to Egypt," the angel told him. "Herod is looking for the baby and wants to kill him. Go quickly. There is no time to lose. In Egypt, you will be safe."

Jesus woke Mary. Quickly, they wrapped baby Jesus in a warm blanket, collected up their belongings and crept out of Bethlehem. It took them many days to reach Egypt but at last they were safe from harm. And there they stayed until the angel visited Joseph again and told him that Herod was dead. Then it was safe for Joseph, Mary and Jesus to go home to Nazareth.

Pictures
Page 18: *Choir boys sing traditional Christmas carols at a service in Westminster Abbey, London.*
Page 19: *A little girl opens her presents under a Christmas tree on Christmas Day.*

Christmas stained glass windows

Group of up to 6 children

You will need:
- tissue paper - various colours
- sticky-backed plastic
- black card or thick paper
- photographs of stained glass windows

Beforehand:
1. Cut the sticky-backed plastic into rectangles, about 8 x 10cm.
Attach to the table where the child will be working with re-usable adhesive, so that the sticky side will be upwards when the protective backing paper is taken off.

2. Cut the black card into rectangles about the same shape as the sticky-backed plastic. Cut a Christmas shape in the middle of each piece - a star, a Christmas tree, etc.

3. Tear the tissue paper into long, thin strips.

Activity
If possible, take the children on a visit to a church to see the stained glass windows. If this is not possible, show them some photographs.

Explain that the children are going to make a stained glass window. Help them peel off the protective backing from the sticky-backed plastic. Show them how to tear the tissue into small pieces and place flat onto the sticky-backed plastic. Encourage the children to use different colours and to think about the stained glass windows they have just seen in the church or in the photos. Encourage the children not to stick tissue paper around the very edge of the sticky-backed plastic.

When the children are satisfied that they have enough tissue on their sticky-backed plastic, ask them to choose a window shape and place it on top of the sticky-backed plastic so that the tissue becomes the 'glass'. Stick the finished artwork on to a window for the light to shine through.

Extensions
- The child can tear the tissue into lengths and then into small pieces.
- The child makes a pattern with the tissue.

Support
- Tear the tissue into small pieces beforehand.

Early Learning Goals
- Observe, find out about and identify features in the place they live.

Wrapping presents
Group of up to 4 children

You will need:
- boxes of assorted sizes
- Christmas paper cut into different sizes
- sticky tape - a roll for each child if possible
- scissors for each child

Discuss with the children why we give each other presents at Christmas - remind them of the presents that the three wise men brought for Jesus. Discuss how it feels to give and to be given a present.

Tell the children that you need some boxes wrapped to look like presents to decorate the room.

Show the children how to wrap a box, by demonstrating one of your own very slowly.

Ask each child to choose a box and to find a piece of wrapping paper that is big enough to wrap the box in. Help them wrap the paper round the boxes and fold in the corners.

Show the children how to stick the sticky tape to the table, pull it out and cut the required length off.

Extension
• Turn the role play area into Santa's Grotto and have present-making and wrapping activities.

Support
• Cut the sticky tape ready for use and place in a convenient place for the children to use.

Early Learning Goals
• Use developing mathematical ideas to solve practical problems.
• Consider the consequences of their words and actions for themselves and others.

Making snowflakes
Group of up to 6 children

You will need:
• red/black card A4 size
• small doilies
• white paint
• paint rollers
• masking tape

Beforehand:
Attach the doilies to the card with a small bit of masking tape. Do extra as the children will undoubtedly want to do more than one of these.

Give each child a piece of card with a doily stuck on and let them roll white paint over the doily. Help them remove the doily to see the snowflake pattern they have made on the card. Hang the snowflakes up around the room as Christmas decorations.

Extension
• Show the children how to attach the doily to the card so that they can make as many as they like.

Early Learning Goal
• Handle tools safely and with increasing control.

Santa calendars
Group of up to 6 children

You will need:
• thick piece of A4 card for each child
• pink paper
• red felt
• cotton wool
• wiggly eyes
• glue sticks
• red felt pens
• small 10 x 5cm calendars for the coming year

Beforehand:
Cut the pink paper into circles for Santa's face so that they fit in the centre of the A4 card, leaving enough room for a hat and a beard. Cut the felt into triangles for Santa's hat, making sure they fit the pink paper circle.

Activity
Explain to the children that they are going to make a calendar present for someone they love. Give each child a piece of the card, and let them stick a pink paper circle in the middle of it.

Let them choose two eyes to stick on the face, and they can draw on Santa's mouth with a red felt pen. Let them choose a red triangle to stick on as Santa's hat, and cotton wool to stick on as a beard and hair. Finally, give them a small calendar to stick on to the bottom of the card.

Early Learning Goal
• Demonstrate fine motor control and co-ordination.

The Story of Easter

Long ago, Jesus and his friends went to Jerusalem. Jesus wanted to teach the people there about God. Jesus rode into the city on a donkey. Crowds of people came to meet him. Some of them laid their cloaks on the ground for the donkey to walk over. Other people waved long, green palm leaves. They were very happy to see Jesus and wanted to welcome him.

Jesus was glad to see so many people. But he also felt sad. He knew that his life was in danger because his enemies in Jerusalem did not like what he taught. They wanted to get rid of him, as quickly as they could.

A few days later, Jesus sat down with his friends to eat a meal. Jesus's friends laughed and joked. They were happy to be together. But they noticed that Jesus looked tired and sad.

"What is the matter, master?" one of Jesus's friends asked him. "Why do you look so sad?"

"I have something to tell you," Jesus said, quietly. The friends fell silent.

"This is the last time I will share a meal with you," Jesus told them.

Then Jesus picked up some bread. He blessed it and broke it into pieces. He gave a piece to each of his friends.

"Whenever you eat bread," he said, "you should remember me."

Then Jesus picked up a cup of wine and passed it round the table. Each of his friends took a sip.

"Whenever you drink wine," he said, "you should remember me."

Jesus's friends were frightened. They did not understand what Jesus meant. Why was this their last meal together? What was going to happen? They loved Jesus very much and did not want him to leave them.

Later that night, Jesus and his friends went to a garden to pray. Jesus did not notice that there were soldiers hiding among the trees.

One of Jesus's friends was called Judas. When no one was looking, he crept up to the soldiers.

"I can show you who Jesus is," Judas whispered. "I will give him a kiss."

Then Judas went up to Jesus and kissed him on the cheek. This was the sign that the soldiers had been waiting for. At once, they grabbed Jesus and dragged him away. Then they threw him into prison. The next day, they fetched Jesus and took him to see the ruler of Jerusalem. His name was

Pontius Pilate. Pilate listened to Jesus's enemies. They told him that Jesus was a troublemaker. Then Pilate ordered that Jesus be killed.

On Good Friday, Jesus was taken away to a nearby hill. He was nailed to a wooden cross and left to die. Even though Jesus was in great pain, he asked God to forgive his enemies for what they had done to him.

Later that day, Jesus died. Gently, some of Jesus's friends took his body down from the cross. They wrapped the body in a white robe and put it in a tomb cut into a rock. Then they rolled a big stone across the entrance. Jesus's friends were crying. It was the saddest day of their lives. They thought that they would never see Jesus again.

Two days later, some of Jesus's friends went back to visit the tomb. But when they got there, they could not believe their eyes. The stone had been rolled away. And when they looked inside the tomb, it was empty!

"What has happened?" they wondered. "Where has Jesus gone?"

Then they saw a shining angel, standing by the tomb.

"Don't be afraid," the angel said. "I have some good news for you. I know that you are looking for Jesus. But he is not here. Jesus is not dead anymore. He has come back to life."

Jesus's friends were very happy. But they were also afraid. They missed Jesus very much. But what if the news was too good to be true? How could Jesus have come back to life? After all, they had seen him die. Quickly, they ran to tell the others what had happened. But on the way, an amazing thing happened. A man was walking along the road towards them. And the man was Jesus!

The friends saw Jesus several more times after that. He told them to go everywhere they could to teach people all about God. Then Jesus went up to Heaven to be with God.

Pictures
Page 24: *The Paschal, or Easter, candle is lit in many Christian churches late on Holy Saturday (Easter eve). It is a symbol of Jesus as a light in the darkness.*
Page 25: *Eggs are traditionally given at Easter to celebrate the spring and new life. These eggs have been painted with bright colours and patterns.*

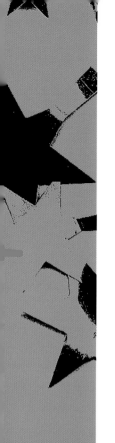

Chocolate nests

Group of up to 6 children

You will need:
- plain/milk chocolate bars
- crispy rice cereal
- packets of mini-eggs
- a plastic knife for each child
- a large saucepan
- a wooden spoon
- paper cases

Explain to the children that Easter comes in the spring when the Earth is getting warmer after winter, animals are having babies, and birds are making nests ready to lay their eggs in.

Explain that we give each other eggs at Easter because of the new life that happens at this time of year.

Give each child some chocolate to break or cut into small pieces and put into the saucepan. Discuss what the chocolate feels like and what might happen when you heat the saucepan. Let the children each stir the chocolate lumps.

An adult should heat the chocolate until it melts, then let the children stir again. Discuss how the chocolate has changed. Let each child add a spoonful of crispy rice cereal until the chocolate is used up coating the cereal.

Give each child a paper case and let them spoon some 'nest' mixture into it. Make a little hollow for the eggs to sit in. Let each child count out 3 eggs to put in their nest.

Early Learning Goals
- Count reliably up to 10 everyday objects.
- Use talk to organise, sequence and clarify thinking ideas, feelings and events.
- Look closely at similarities, differences, patterns and change.

Make an Easter bunny mask

Group of up to 4 children

You will need:
- a small paper plate for each child
- colouring pencils
- card
- stapler
- cotton wool balls
- glue
- pipe cleaners
- elastic

Beforehand:
Cut two ears for each child from the card.

Activity
Give each child a paper plate and tell them they are going to make an Easter bunny mask. Get the children to turn their plates upside down.

Let the children colour their plates while you go to each child in turn and ask them to count out two ears each. Help them to staple the ears onto the plate. Cut eye holes in each plate.

Let the children glue a cotton wool ball on to the plate for the rabbit's nose, and add whiskers made of pipe cleaners.

Allow to dry.

When the rabbit masks are dry, attach elastic so the children can wear them.

Extensions
- Sing rabbit songs with the children wearing their masks such as 'See the little bunnies sleeping'.
- Create a rabbit burrow in the role play area or outside and let the children be a rabbit family wearing their masks.

Support
- Make only the ears if a child does not like wearing a mask. Staple ears onto a band that fits around the child's head.

Card matching game

Group of up to 6 children

You will need:
- old Easter cards
- bowl of little Easter eggs

Beforehand:
Cut all the cards into half using a variety of zigzag/wiggly cuts. Hide one half of each card around the room - preferably where the children won't see them until you want them to.

Activity
Show the children the card halves in your hand. Explain that you have lost the other half of each card, and that you need their help to find them.

Give each child half of a card and send them off to find the other half. When they have matched the halves together, get them to put them on the table beside their name. Give the child a new half. Do this until all the cards have been matched.

The children count up how many whole cards they have found.

At the end of the game, you could give each child a couple of little eggs.

Extensions
- Teach the children that two halves make one card - how many halves do they have? How many whole cards do they have?
- Cut the cards into 3 or 4 pieces.

Support
- Hide the whole card so that the children are just looking for any card.

Early Learning Goal
- Count reliably up to 10 everyday objects.

Make an Easter basket

Group of up to 6 children

You will need:
- a polystyrene cup for each child
- pipe cleaners
- egg shapes cut from card
- stickers/sequins etc.
- glue
- green tissue paper
- pens

Let the children decorate their cups by gluing decorations on the outside. Help each child make a hole in each side of the cup and thread a pipe cleaner through to act as a handle.

Ask each child to tear little pieces of tissue to put in their cup as grass. Then get them to count out five eggs each. They should colour the eggs and put them into their basket.

Extensions
- Number the eggs 1-5. The children must pick out one of each.
- The children cut out egg shapes to go into their baskets.

Early Learning Goals
- Demonstrate fine motor control and co-ordination.
- Use their imagination in art and design.

מצה
MATZAH

בּיצה
Egg

Shank Bone

חזרת
Horse Radish

פסח

מרור
Bitter Herbs

כרפס
Parsley

חרוסת
Haroseth

The Story of Pesach

Many, many years ago, the Jewish people lived in Egypt. For a while, their lives were happy. But then a new king came to the throne. He did not like the Jews and forced them to work as slaves. The king made the Jews build the royal cities and palaces. It was hard work, and the Jews were tired and miserable. But they did their work as well as they could and never complained. This made the king very angry.

One day, the cruel king gave an order.

"Go to every Jewish home," he told his soldiers. "Take away all the baby boys. Then throw them in the river!"

At about this time, a Jewish woman had a baby boy. She loved him very much and did not want the soldiers to find him. So she made a basket from bulrushes and gently laid her baby inside. Then she hid the basket among the reeds by the riverbank.

Later that day, the Egyptian king's daughter came to swim in the river. She found the basket. Inside, there was a baby boy and he was crying.

"Don't cry, little baby," the king's daughter said. "I will look after you."

So she took the baby home and brought him up as her own son. She called him Moses.

Moses grew up in the royal palace. He was treated like a prince. But he never forgot his Jewish roots. Then, one day, Moses heard a voice calling to him. It was the voice of God.

"Moses!" said God. "I have seen how unhappy my people are. And I have come to save them. I have chosen you to be the leader of the Jews. Go to the king and tell him to set the Jews free. Then lead them out of Egypt."

Moses did as God asked. He went to speak to the king of Egypt.

"Your majesty," he said. "Please let the Jewish people go."

But the king refused. "I will never let the Jewish people go," he said. "They can work harder than ever instead."

Again and again, Moses went to the king and asked him to let the Jews go. But every time, the king said no.

✡

So God decided to punish the king and the Egyptians. He sent ten terrible plagues to Egypt. First, the water in all of the rivers turned into blood. Then frogs appeared everywhere. Then lice fell from the sky, and fierce wild beasts roamed all over the land. Next, God sent a horrible disease that killed the Egyptians' farm animals. Then people were covered in painful boils. Then came huge hailstones which flattened the crops in the fields. Next, swarms of locusts ate all the crops. Then it was dark for three whole days. No wonder the people of Egypt were terrified.

Even after all of this, the king of Egypt did not change his mind. He still refused to set the Jews free. Then God sent a tenth plague – the most terrible of all. The eldest boy in every Egyptian family died, even the king's own son.

✡

After this plague, the Egyptian king called for Moses. "Take your people," he told Moses. "The Jews are free to go. I do not want any more of these terrible plagues."

So the Jews quickly packed up their belongings. Then they followed Moses out of Egypt and into the desert. They did not know which way to go. But God helped the Jews. He sent a cloud to show them the way by day, and a fire to guide them at night.

The king of Egypt let the Jews leave. But then he changed his mind. He sent his army after the Jews to catch them and bring them back to Egypt. The Jews found that they were trapped. In front of them lay a huge, deep lake called the Red Sea. Behind them were the Egyptian soldiers. The Jews could not go forward across the sea. And they could not go back!

But God came to their rescue. He sent a strong wind that blew the water in the lake apart. Now the Jews could walk across the bed of the lake to safety! But when the Egyptian soldiers tried to follow the Jews, the water rushed back again and the soldiers were all drowned.

✡

The Jews lived in the desert for many years. There were many difficult and dangerous times. But God always looked after them. At last, they reached the land of Israel. This was the land that God had promised to them as their home.

Pictures
Page 30: *Each of the foods on a Seder plate is a symbol of the Jews' flight from Egypt. They include bitter herbs, a reminder of the bitterness of slavery, a green vegetable as a sign of new life and a lamb bone as an offering to God.*
Page 31: *At the Seder meal, a boy reads out the story of Pesach from a book called the Haggadah. As the story is read, people taste the different foods on the Seder plate.*

Moses the baby
Circle time - whole group

Tell a simple version of the story.

Wrap a doll in a blanket and place in a basket or small box. Tell the children this is Moses, and you are being his mother. Ask them how they think you and your husband feel sending your baby away. What might Moses need with him in the basket? What can he see from his basket floating down the river? What can he hear? What do the children think he would like to play with? Ask the children one at a time to find Moses something for his basket, and ask them why he would want it.

Leave the doll, basket and things the children have found available for the children to play with.

Extensions
• Discuss how the king's daughter feels when she finds the baby in the reeds.
• Children draw a picture of Moses in his basket.
• Children act out the story, taking the parts of Moses' mother and father, and the king's daughter.

Support
• Talk about what babies need. How do we look after them? Do the children need the same things as babies? What don't they need? What else do they need?

Early Learning Goals
• Have a developing awareness of their own needs, views and feelings and be sensitive to the needs, views and feelings of others.
• Interact with others, negotiating plans and activities and learning to take turns in conversation.
• Sustain attentive listening, responding to what they have heard by relevant comments, questions, or actions.

Matzah pizzas
Group of up to 6 children

You will need:
• a matzah (large square cracker) for each child
• cheese, tomatoes, spring onions – desired toppings
• plastic knives
• chopping boards or plates
• a grill

Explain to the children that Jewish people eat matzot during Passover because when they had to leave Egypt quickly, they had no time to let their bread rise. They had to bake it quickly and take it like that. Matzot are like the unrisen bread.

Give each child a plastic knife and a chopping board or plate. Allow them to select the food they like and cut it into small pieces.

Give each child a matzah and get them to spread their chopped food on the matzah, finishing with the cheese.

An adult grills the pizzas. Ask the children to observe any changes that take place during grilling.

Extension
• Make a tomato sauce topping with chopped onions, tinned tomatoes and herbs, etc.

Support
• Pre-chop the vegetables and let the child sprinkle them on the matzah.

Early Learning Goals
• Handle tools with increasing control.
• Look closely at similarities, differences and change.

Hunt for Hametz

(This would be a good activity to do on the day before Pesach begins.)

Whole group activity

You will need:
• bread, buns - anything with yeast in
• matzot
• pitta bread
• cling film

Beforehand:
Wrap slices of bread and buns in cling film and hide around the classroom.

Activity
Show the children the bread, matzot, pitta bread and buns. How do they differ from each other? Show how flat the matzot and pittas are, and how the bread is big and more puffed up because of the yeast that has been used to make it.

Explain to the children that Jewish people are not allowed to eat yeast during Pesach, because in the old story the Jews had to leave Egypt quickly and had no time to let their bread rise so they baked it quickly and took it unrisen. So they cannot eat bread and buns and eat matzot instead during Pesach.

Explain to the children that on the evening before the festival of Pesach begins, Jewish children hunt around the house for any foods that are not allowed during Pesach.

Tell the children that you have hidden some bread and buns called 'hametz' (forbidden food) around the classroom for them to try to find.

When the children have found all the bread and buns, have a 'day before Pesach' snack of bread, buns and jam.

Early Learning Goal
• Look closely at similarities, differences, patterns and change.

Pesach collage
Group of up to 6 children

You will need:
• large paper plates
• collage material that could represent Pesach food, for example - broken matzot, wet sand (charoset), torn-up green tissue paper, yellow and white circles (egg)
• a small jar of salt water coloured red (wine and salt water)
• two eye droppers
• PVA glue and glue sticks

Explain to the children that Jewish people eat special food at Pesach. During each explanation, show them the collage material that can be used to represent the food.

1. Matzot - this is like the bread that didn't have time to rise.

2. Eggs - to represent new life.

3. Charoset - a paste of nuts, apples, cinnamon and wine - this is like the mortar used to build the Jewish houses.

4. Greenery (they usually eat lettuce) - this shows new life.

5. Salt water - ask the children what their tears taste of. Explain that the salt water at Pesach is like the tears that the Jews cried when they were slaves.

6. Wine - this is to show how God promised the Jewish people that they would be free.

(A Seder plate also traditionally includes bitter herbs to remind Jews of the bitterness of slavery, and a lamb bone. See page 33.)

Tell the children they are going to make a plate of Pesach food. Give them a paper plate and allow them to make their meal. Let them use the eye droppers to drop a small amount of 'wine' over the meal.

Early Learning Goals
• Explore colour, texture, shape, form and space in two or three dimensions.
• Use their imagination in art and design.

Judaism: Hanukkah

The Story of Hanukkah

A powerful king, called King Antiochus, once ruled over a large kingdom. King Antiochus was Greek and he worshipped the Greek gods. He wanted everyone in his kingdom to worship them too. So he sent out an order, telling people to give up their own religious beliefs.

Most people in the kingdom did as the king asked. Only the Jews did not obey him. They wanted to follow their own religion and to pray to their own god. King Antiochus was furious. He was used to people doing what he told them to do. He decided to punish the Jews for refusing to obey his orders.

King Antiochus tried to stop the Jews following their religion. He stopped them reading their holy books. He stopped them praying and resting on the Sabbath, their holy day. Then he sent his soldiers to the Temple in Jerusalem. This was a very special place where the Jews worshipped God. The soldiers smashed the Temple pots and jars. They stole the Temple treasures. A special lamp always burned in the Temple to show that God was there. The soldiers put it out. In its place, they set up statues of the Greek gods.

The king ordered the Jews to worship these gods instead of their own.

"And woe betide anyone who does not obey my order," he said. "They will be killed."

Even so, some brave Jews still stood up for what they believed in. In a small town, not far from Jerusalem, there lived an old priest, called Mattathias. He and his five sons refused to obey King Antiochus. They pulled down the statues of the Greek gods which had been put up in their town. This put their lives in danger and they ran away to the hills to hide. Soon, more and more Jews joined them. They all wanted to stay true to God and they were ready to risk their lives for him. When old Mattathias died, one of his sons became leader of the Jews. His name was Judah. He made the Jews into a small army.

"We must be ready to fight for our freedom," he told them.

When the king heard what was going on, he was furious. He decided to punish the Jews once and for all. So he put together a huge army. Then he led his soldiers into battle against the Jews.

When they saw the king's huge army, the Jews were very frightened.

"Look at all those soldiers," they said. "Our army is so small. We don't stand a chance against them."

But Judah would not let his men get downhearted. "Yes, the king's army is big," he told them. "And ours is small. But we are fighting for God. He will look after us."

And so the battle began. Judah's army fought very bravely against the Greeks. The Jews won a great victory. It seemed that God was truly on the side of the Jews. He watched over them and kept them safe from harm.

After that, the Jews won many more battles against the king's soldiers. In time, they forced their Greek enemies to leave Jerusalem. Then Judah led the Jews into their holy city. They went to the Temple to thank God for their victory. But a terrible sight met their eyes. Everything in the Temple had been destroyed by the soldiers.

"The first thing we must do," Judah told the Jews, "is mend all the damage that has been done to our Temple."

So the Jews set to work. First, they removed the statues of the Greek gods. Then they swept up the broken pots and jars and cleaned the Temple from top to bottom.

"Now we must light the Temple lamp," Judah said, "to celebrate our victory. Then the Temple will be holy once more."

The Jews looked everywhere for some oil to light the lamp. But they could not find any. Every jar of oil in the Temple had been broken and the oil spilt. At last, Judah found a single jar of oil which had been hidden in a corner. But the jar was almost empty. There was just enough oil left in it to keep the lamp burning for one day. What was Judah going to do?

Judah took the oil he had found and used it to light the Temple lamp. To his amazement, the lamp did not go out at the end of the day. Instead, it kept on burning for eight whole days. This gave the Jews enough time to fetch some more oil.

"God has helped us," said Judah. "A great miracle has happened here."

Pictures
Page 36: *A girl lights the candles on a special candlestick called a hanukiah. The eight candles stand for the eight nights of Hanukkah. The ninth candle is used to light them with.*
Page 37: *After each candle is lit, special prayers and blessings are said to thank God for the miracle of Hanukkah. The candlestick is then displayed in a window so that everyone can see it.*

Cooking potato and apple latkes
Group of up to 6 children

Jews eat latkes (potato pancakes) at Hanukkah because they are cooked in oil and so remind them of the miracle of the single jar of oil.

You will need (for 10 pancakes):

• 500g potatoes
• 1 apple
• 1 large egg
• 30g flour
• salt
• ground pepper
• oil for frying
• sugar
• a grater or food processor
• a frying pan or deep fat fryer
• a potato peeler
• weighing scales
• a large mixing bowl
• a muslin or tea towel
• a wooden spoon
• a spatula
• paper towels

Throughout this activity, talk with the children about what is happening to the ingredients. What pattern does the grater make on the potato? How is the inside of the apple different from the outside? Does the apple look/feel/smell the same as the potato? etc.

Help the children weigh and count out the ingredients.

Help the children peel the potatoes (a Swiss style peeler held in one hand and pulled down the length of the vegetable is easier for children to manage than one held sideways).

Help the children grate the potatoes and apples or supervise them using the food processor.

It is very important to get the liquid out of the potatoes and apples, so when they are all grated, put them into a muslin or tea towel and squeeze hard to remove the liquid. This is a good exercise for the children to build up the muscles in their hands in preparation for pencil control.

Put the grated potatoes and apples in a bowl and mix in all ingredients except oil. Stir well.

Ask the children to describe the mixture, and count how many pancakes are needed.

An adult then cooks the pancakes.

In a large non-stick frying pan, heat enough oil to cover the bottom of the pan. Spoon out the batter into the pan. Cook until crisp and brown on one side, then turn and fry on the other side. Keep finished pancakes warm in the oven until all pancakes are fried. Drain on paper towels. Sprinkle with sugar if desired just before serving.

Early Learning Goal
• Look closely at similarities, differences, patterns and change.

Making a dreidel
Group of up to 6 children

You will need:
• a small box for each child
• plain white paper - the right size to cover the boxes
• glue sticks
• colouring pencils

Explain to the children that Jewish people play a traditional game at Hanukkah with a sort of spinning top called a dreidel. The children are going to make a similar game.

Give each child a box and some white paper. Show them how to put glue on the box and then stick the paper on to cover it. Trim the paper so that it is neat.

Give the children one coloured pencil and ask them to draw on one face of the box. Get them to draw with a different colour on each face.

Play a game - help the children to decide what each colour means (e.g. blue means sit down, green means jump up and down, etc.)

Choose one child to roll their dreidel. All the children do the action for the colour that the dreidel turns up.

Extensions
• Use numbers instead of colours and get the child who rolls the dreidel to decide what action to do before s/he rolls. They perform that action the number of times that the dreidel tells them to.
• Use letters - when the dreidel lands they think up a word beginning with that letter.

Support
• Use wax crayons to colour.
• Play a game rolling the dreidel and naming the colour that lands upwards.

Early Learning Goals
• Explore colour, shape, form in 3 dimensions.
• Use language to describe the shape and size of solids.

Counting the hanukiah
Group of up to 6 children

You will need:
• a photocopy of a hanukiah for each child
• yellow paper or card
• glue sticks
• a candle

Beforehand:
From the yellow paper/card, cut out 9 flame shapes for each child, so that the flames fit onto the hanukiah on the photocopied sheets.

Activity
Explain that Jewish people light a candlestick called a hanukiah at Hanukkah. Show them a picture of the hanukiah and count the candles. Explain that Jewish people display the hanukiah in their window during Hanukkah time.

Explain that the festival of Hanukkah lasts for 8 days. That is why there should be 8 candles.

But there are 9. Why are there 9? Listen to the children's ideas and then explain that one candle is used to light all the other candles. This candle is called the 'shamash' or 'servant' candle.

Use the candle to demonstrate how an adult would use the servant candle to light all the others.

Give each child a photocopy of the hanukiah and ask them to count out 9 of the cut-out flames each.

Show them how to arrange the flames on each candle and stick them on to light their hanukiah.

Extensions
• Number the candles on the photocopy and the flames, so that the children need to stick each flame on its matching candle.
• Children write the numbers on the candles.

Early Learning Goals
• Count reliably up to 10 everyday objects.
• Recognise numerals 1-9.

Eid Mubarak

The Story of Id-ul-Adha

Long ago, the Prophet Ibrahim lived happily with his two wives, Sarah and Hajar. He also had a son called Isma'il, whom he loved very much. The Prophet Ibrahim was a very holy man. He was known as the Friend of Allah (God). He spent his life praising Allah and living a good life, as Allah wanted him to.

One night, Ibrahim had a strange dream. He dreamt that Allah told him to kill his beloved son, Isma'il. Ibrahim was very sad. Isma'il was only ten years old. Why would Allah want Ibrahim to kill him? But Ibrahim went to find Isma'il and told him what Allah had said in his dream.

"Dear father," said Isma'il. "Do not be sad. We must follow Allah's wishes and do what he wants us to do."

So Ibrahim took Isma'il to Mina, a place near to the holy city of Makkah. This was where he would follow Allah's wishes and kill Isma'il, his son.

But on the way to Mina, their path was blocked by a sinister-looking stranger. Ibrahim and Isma'il did not know it, but the stranger was the Devil in disguise.

"Where are you going?" the stranger asked them.

"We are going to follow Allah's wishes," Ibrahim replied.

"But surely Allah is good and kind?" said the stranger. "He would not want you to kill your son. That must be the work of the Devil. Now, why don't you go home and forget all about this?"

But Ibrahim now saw that this was the Devil. And he did not listen to what he said. He carried on on his way. But the Devil did not give up. Next, he turned to Isma'il.

"Did you know," he said to Isma'il, "that your father is planning to kill you? What do you think of that?"

"If that is what Allah wants him to do," replied Isma'il, "then he must follow Allah's wishes."

Still, the Devil did not give up. For a third time, he tried to stop Ibrahim and Isma'il from following Allah's wishes. He went to speak to Hajar, Isma'il's mother.

"Did you know," he said to Hajar, "that your husband is planning to kill your son? Surely you should stop him?"

But, like Ibrahim and Isma'il, Hajar would not listen to the Devil.

"If that is what Allah wants him to do," she replied, "then Ibrahim must follow Allah's wishes."

Then Ibrahim and Isma'il picked up a handful of stones. They threw them at the Devil to drive him away.

Now the time had come for the greatest test. It was time for Ibrahim to kill Isma'il, his much-loved son. Ibrahim picked up his knife.

"I am so sorry, my dear son," he said, with tears in his eyes.

"I have promised to obey Allah in everything I do. And I must follow Allah's wishes, even in this."

But just as Ibrahim was about to sacrifice Isma'il, the knife was twisted out of his hand. It fell to the ground with a clatter. Ibrahim looked around, but he could not see anyone. Then he heard Allah's voice calling to him.

"Oh, Ibrahim," the voice said. "You do not need to kill your son. You have already shown how much you love me. You were ready to obey me, even if it meant losing the most precious thing in your life. Now sacrifice this ram instead of Isma'il."

So Ibrahim and Isma'il killed the ram which Allah had sent instead, just as Allah had told them to.

Pictures
Page 42: *These girls are dressed up in their best clothes to celebrate the joyful festival of Id-ul-Adha.*
Page 43: *At Id, many Muslims exchange greeting cards. They are decorated with beautiful patterns and the words 'Id Mubarak' or 'Happy Id'.*

Page 48: *On the morning of Id-ul-Fitr, Muslims attend the mosque for Id prayers. They praise Allah and thank him for giving them the strength to fast throughout Ramadan.*
Page 49: *At the end of Id-ul-Fitr, Muslims celebrate with a special meal to mark the end of Ramadan. During Ramadan, they fast from daybreak to sunset.*

Mosque collage
Whole group

You will need:
• card cut into different mosque shapes
• glue sticks
• photos of different shaped mosques
• sequins and sparkly bits

Ideally, take the children to see a mosque before doing this activity. If you cannot visit a mosque, show the children photos of mosques. Talk about the shape of mosques and ask the children if they have seen/been in a mosque.

Explain to the children that they are going to brighten up some mosque shapes ready for Id-ul-Adha festival.

Ask each child to choose a mosque shape and decorate with sequins etc.

Extensions
• Talk about what happens in a mosque - compare with other places of worship.
• Build up a collection of labelled photos of different religious buildings.

Sharing money
Group of up to 6 children

You will need:
• small envelopes
• real pennies
• number cards 1-5 in a basket

Beforehand:
Put pennies into the envelopes - vary the amounts, but put a minimum of one and maximum of 5 in each envelope. Seal the envelopes.

Activity
Explain to the children that Muslims give presents and money to people who do not have as much as themselves. They do this especially during festivals.

Ask each child to choose an envelope, open it and count the pennies inside.

Get them to choose the number card that matches the number of pennies they have.

Then ask them to share their pennies around, for example say, "Ahmed, please can you give two of your pennies to George… Lisa can you give one penny to Kaitlin…" and so on.

When they have done as you asked, ask them to count their pennies again. How many have they got now? Is the number card they have the right one, or do they need to change it?

Repeat the game as many times as the children want.

Extension
• Increase the number of pennies and the numbers on the number cards.

Support
• Have dots on the number cards.

Early Learning Goals
• Recognise numerals 1-5.
• Relates addition to combining two groups of objects.
• Relates subtraction to taking away.

Going on a journey
Group of up to 10 children

You will need:
• photos of pilgrims at Makkah
• variety of clothes for hot and cold weather
• a small suitcase
• two strips of white cloth

Explain to the children that every year many Muslims go on a long journey called a pilgrimage, to a place called Makkah. They call the journey the Hajj. Show the children photos of the pilgrims at Makkah. Discuss the photos with the children - what are the pilgrims wearing? What do they think the weather is like?

Ask the children what they would need to pack if they were going to Makkah. Show them the variety of clothes and get them, one by one, to choose an item of clothing to put into the suitcase.

Show the children the two strips of white cloth (called an ihram), and explain that Muslims drape these over themselves when they arrive in Makkah. Explain that pilgrims on the Hajj wear simple, white clothes to show that they are all equal.

Once the suitcase is packed with all the necessary items, ask the children if they have a special thing that they would take on a journey with them.

Role-play going on a journey - let the children decide where to go and how to travel.

Extensions
• Write a story about the journey you role play as a class activity - let the children illustrate a page each.
• Discuss different ways of travelling. Show the children where Makkah is on a globe, and where they live. If they wanted to get to Makkah, would they need to cross any seas? Show them the seas on the globe.

Early Learning Goals
• Use talk to clarify thinking ideas, feelings and events.
• Use their imagination in role play.

Planning an Id-ul-Adha party
Up to 6 children

You will need:
• pen and paper

Explain to the children a day or so before you plan the party that Muslims wear their best clothes for the festival of Id-ul-Adha and share a special feast with family and friends.

Explain that your group is going to have a small Id-ul-Adha party. What would they wear? Get them to describe the clothes they like the best. Write the descriptions down. Ask them what they would like to eat at the party.

Send a note out to parents, saying something like: "The group is having a small party to celebrate the festival of Id-ul-Adha on (date). I have decided that I would like to wear (child's description of clothes), and would like to bring (description of food child has chosen)."

Get the child to write their name on the letter.

Extension
• Invite parents and friends to the party - children design the invitations.

Support
• Write the child's name and let them decorate the letter.

Early Learning Goals
• Write their own names.
• Interact with others, negotiating plans and taking turns in conversation.

Islam: Id-ul-Fitr

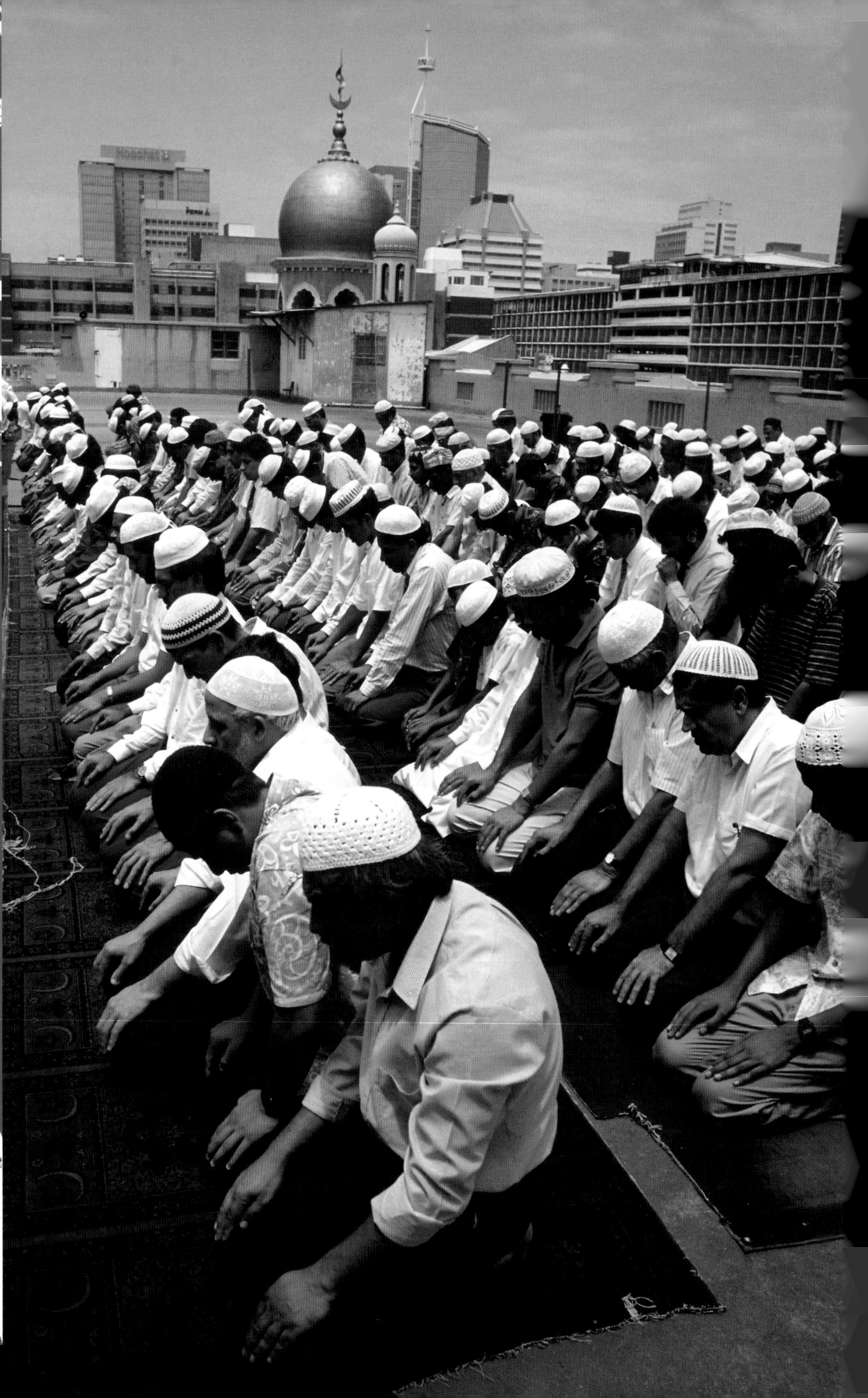

Make a mobile
Group activity for up to 6 children

You will need:
• a large cut-out of a crescent moon for each child on black card
• a large cut-out of a star for each child on black card
• sequins, glitter, sparkly material etc.
• glue
• wool or coloured string

Explain to the children that the festival of Id-ul-Fitr begins when a new moon appears in the sky. For many days before this new moon, Muslims have been fasting. They do not drink or eat during the day for a whole month. This is called Ramadan. Id-ul-Fitr marks the end of Ramadan, so Muslims wait for the new moon eagerly.

Show the children a crescent moon and explain that this is what the new moon looks like.

Give each child a moon and a star to decorate, using glue to stick sequins and sparkly bits on.

Help the children punch one hole in the top and one hole in the bottom of their moon and one hole in the top of their star with a hole puncher.

Help the children cut some wool or string and tie the star so that it hangs below the moon.

Help the children tie a string to the top of the moon to hang it from the ceiling or wall.

Support
• Children use star stickers to decorate their moons and stars.

Early Learning Goal
• Handle tools and objects safely and with increasing control.

Making a decoration
Group activity for up to 6 children

You will need:
• a twig with several little branches for each child
• a jar or pot for each child
• glue sticks
• silver foil
• cut-out stars or stickers
• old modelling clay

Beforehand:
• Cut the silver foil into strips - about 5cm wide.

Activity
Give each child a twig, a pot and a lump of modelling clay. Ask them to push the modelling clay into the pot and then push their twig into the modelling clay, so that the twig stands up like a little tree.

Show the children how to tear a square of silver foil and gently screw it into a small ball. Use the glue stick to put some glue onto the twig to stick the silver foil 'moon' on. Decorate the whole tree with moons and stars.

Extension
• Use cut-out card stars and crescent moons and tie them onto the twig.

Support
• Use silver and gold star stickers.

A welcome meal
Group of up to 10 children

You will need:
• a paper plate for each child
• pictures of different foods and drinks cut out from magazines
• glue sticks

Explain to the children that Id-ul-Fitr means 'festival of breaking the fast'.

Explain the word 'breakfast'. A fast means going without food. Every day when we have breakfast we are breaking our fast, because we haven't eaten during the night. Explain that, during Ramadan, Muslims do not eat or drink anything during the day. Get the children to close their eyes and imagine not eating or drinking anything all day, as long as there is light in the sky. They would have to get up early to eat their breakfast before the sun came up. Then - no snack time at nursery, no lunch, no snacks in the afternoon until the sun goes down and they are allowed to eat.

Get the children to open their eyes and look at the pictures you have cut out from magazines. Get them to choose what they would feel like eating and drinking after fasting all day.

Ask the children to make a picture of their Ramadan meal and glue it onto their plate.

Early Learning Goal
• Express and communicate their ideas, thoughts and feelings by using a widening range of materials.

Making date and fig bread

Group of up to 6 children

You will need:
• 180g dates
• 200g dried figs
• 55g unsalted butter, softened
• 1-and-a-half teaspoons bicarbonate of soda
• 235ml boiling water
• 100g white sugar
• 2 eggs
• 95g plain flour
• 90g whole wheat flour
• Half-teaspoon baking powder
• Half-teaspoon salt
• scales for weighing ingredients
• 2 large mixing bowls
• plastic knife for each child
• a large spoon for mixing
• 20 x 10cm baking tin

Preheat the oven to 350°F (175°C/ gas mark 4). Help the children weigh out the ingredients. As the dried fruit is weighed, let some of the children chop it up.

Give another child the job of greasing the baking tin.

Help the children mix dates, figs, butter and bicarbonate of soda.

Adult pours in the boiling water, all stir well and leave to stand. While this is standing, help the children break the eggs into the other mixing bowl, and add the sugar. All beat well. Add the two flours, baking powder and salt.

Stir all this into the date mixture until blended. Pour the batter into the baking tin.

Throughout this activity, encourage the children to talk about the ingredients using their senses. Discuss the smell and feel of the dates, the look of the mixture and how it changes, and introduce vocabulary such as heavier, lighter, etc.

Adult puts the pan in the oven to bake for 55-60 minutes, or until a knife inserted into the middle of the loaf comes out clean. Allow to cool in the pan for 10 minutes, then turn out onto a wire rack to cool completely. Eat for snack time or cut up for children to take home.

Early Learning Goals
• In practical activities and discussion, begin to use the vocabulary involved in adding and subtracting.
• Use language such as 'greater' 'lighter' 'smaller' 'heavier' to compare quantities.
• Look closely at similarities, differences, patterns and change.

The Story of Divali

There was once a king called King Dasharatha who ruled a kingdom in India. He was a good king who ruled wisely and well. Prince Rama was the eldest of the king's four sons. He was brave and handsome, and his father's favourite. Rama married a beautiful princess, called Sita.

King Dasharatha was very proud of his son. "Rama will be king after me," he told his wife, Rama's stepmother.

But his wife had other plans. She also had a son, called Bharat, and she wanted him to be the next king.

"But my lord," she said, "long ago, I saved your life. And you gave me two wishes in return. Now it is time for you to keep your promises. Firstly, I want you to make my son king. And secondly, I want you to send Rama away to live in the forest."

The king was heartbroken. But he had to keep his promises to the queen. So Rama went off to live in the forest. His wife Sita and his brother, Lakshman, went with him.

Many years went by. Rama, Sita and Lakshman lived happily together in a little cottage deep in the forest.

One day, Rama and Lakshman went hunting for a golden deer. Sita thought the golden deer was the most beautiful creature she had ever seen and she wanted to keep one as a pet.

While they were gone, a poor, old man knocked on the cottage door. He was dressed in the robes of a holy man.

"Can you help me?" he asked Sita. "I've been travelling for many days. I'm very tired and hungry."

At once, kind Sita took the holy man in and gave him some food and water. This was the chance he had been waiting for. For this was no holy man. He was really Ravana, the evil ten-headed demon king of Lanka, in disguise. He had sent the golden deer to trick Rama and Lakshman and keep them out of the way.

Ravana kidnapped Sita and bundled her into his chariot. Then he sped off through the skies to his palace in Lanka, far, far away.

"I will marry Sita," Ravana cried. "Then I will rule the world!"

When Rama and Lakshman got back from hunting, they found that Sita had vanished. For days, they searched the forest. But they could not find her anywhere. Then Rama had an idea.

"We'll ask the monkey army for help," he said. "They'll know what to do."

The monkeys searched high and low. They looked all over India. But they could not find Sita. Just as they were about to give up, they saw a very old bird sitting in a tree.

"I know where Sita is," croaked the bird. "Ravana has taken her to Lanka."

Lanka was an island far out in the sea. To reach Sita, they had to cross the water. But how would they do that?

"I will try," said the brave monkey general, Hanuman. He was the son of the god of the wind. With one leap, he jumped over the sea to Lanka.

Hanuman flew to Ravana's palace. Then, quiet as a mouse, he crept inside. He found Sita sitting in a garden. She was delighted to see him.

"Please rescue me," she whispered.

"Don't worry," said Hanuman. "We will soon come back for you."

Then Hanuman sped back over the sea and told Rama that he had found Sita. Rama soon gathered a huge army of monkeys and bears. Together they built a great stone bridge across the sea and marched over it to Lanka.

In Lanka, Ravana was waiting. He sent out his own army of demons and giants to fight Rama.

"And don't come back until they're all dead!" he screeched after them.

A dreadful battle began. It lasted all day and all night. Spears and arrows flew through the air and many brave soldiers were killed. Finally, it was time for Rama to face Ravana. The demon king put on his finest armour, with a helmet on each of his ten heads. Then, with a bloodthirsty shriek, he raced towards Rama in his chariot. But Rama was ready for him. He had a golden bow and arrow which the gods had given to him. Quick as a flash, he took aim and fired. The arrow hit Ravana and he toppled out of his chariot, dead.

As Rama's army of bears and monkeys cheered, Sita came out of the palace. She was very glad to see Rama. At last, Rama and Sita were able to go home to be crowned as king and queen. They rode on the back of a great white swan. And everywhere people lit tiny lamps to show them the way.

Pictures
Page 52: *A Hindu priest makes an offering to the sacred images of Rama and Sita in a mandir to celebrate Divali.*
Page 53: *At Divali, Hindus light small clay lamps, called divas, to guide Rama and Sita safely home from exile. The divas also symbolise the victory of light over darkness, and good over evil.*

A Divali puppet show
Activity for a group of 6/7 children

You will need:
- paper
- coloured pencils
- scissors
- sticky tape

Make two sets of very simple finger puppets of King Dasharatha, his wife (looking angry), Rama, Sita, Lakshman, Hanuman, Ravana (one side a deer, other side a ten-headed monster) out of drawings on paper.

If the activity is for young children, do not make the ten-headed monster too frightening!

Tape one set to fit adult fingers. Tape the other set to fit child fingers (pictures will have to be smaller on these).

Activity
You will need: two sets of finger puppets (see above)

Explain to the children that Divali is a Hindu celebration when Hindus light lots of little lights. Show the children the photos and ask them why they think the Hindus light all the lights. Note down children's ideas.

Tell the children you are going to tell them a very old story that Hindus remember every year at Divali. Tell the story using the adult-size finger puppets.

Go back to the reasons the children gave for the lights before they heard the story - was anybody right or nearly right?

Let the children each choose a character to play and give them that child-sized finger puppet. Tell the story again and let the children act it out with their finger puppets.

Extensions
- Children tell the story on their own and use the finger puppets.
- Put on a finger puppet show for the rest of the class/parents.
- Children act out the story, dress up and make props to enhance the show.
- Children make up a legend of their own.

Support
- Simplify the story to fewer characters and fewer events.

Indian music and painting
Group of 6 children

You will need:
- a CD/tape of Indian music
- a CD/tape player
- photographs of Indian instruments (optional)
- Indian instruments (optional)
- large sheets of paper
- wax crayons

Play a short section of the Indian music to the children. Ask them if they know what instruments are playing. Have they ever seen any Indian instruments? Do they sound the same as instruments they hear on the radio/TV at home? If possible, show the children pictures or real Indian instruments.

Play the music again and ask the children how it made them feel. Does it make them think of anything? Weather? Animals? Dancing? Tell them how it makes you feel and what it makes you think of.

Give each child a large sheet of paper. (I have tried this using a long roll of paper that was given to us, and the children loved lining up alongside this armed with crayons.) Play the music again and ask the children to draw what the music makes them feel.

Extensions
• Children draw a picture of the Rama and Sita story.
• Play the music for the children to dance to.

Support
• Draw with the child, saying "the music makes me feel excited/sad/happy … I want to draw fast/slow/in circles/zigzag because the music sounds like that" etc.

Early Learning Goals
• Express and communicate their ideas, thoughts and feelings by using a widening range of materials.
• Use their imagination in music, dance, and stories.

This is an English song that can be adapted for Divali, Hanukkah etc.

(Sung to the tune 'Here we go round the mulberry bush')

'This is the way we clean the house, clean the house, clean the house
This is the way we clean the house to celebrate Divali/Hanukkah/.'

'This is the way we light the lamp etc. - to celebrate Divali/Hanukkah.
This is the way we greet our friends (hands in prayer position) at Divali.'

Make a divali light
Group of up to 6 children

You will need:
• clay
• clay tools (or playdough tools) and rolling pins
• a small bowl of water - just big enough for children to dip fingers in - a jam jar lid is ideal
• a night light for each child
• paint
• PVA glue
• photographs of Divali lights

What to do:
Allow the children plenty of exploration with clay before doing this activity, so that they are familiar with how to mould and shape it.

Show the children the photograph of the Divali lights and explain that they are going to make a little pot to hold a light, which can be their Divali light.

Show the children how to roll the clay and then use thumbs and fingers to pull up the edges to form a pot. Show them how to dip their fingers into the water and smooth the clay with wet fingers.

Ask the children to place the night light inside their pot to make sure it is the right size. Decorate the pot with clay tools and allow to dry.

When dry, children paint the pots using paint mixed with PVA glue to give it a varnished look and feel.

Place the night light inside.

Discuss with the children the dangers of matches and how the night light must only be lit by an adult, and put in a safe place while it is alight.

Extensions
• Make a coil pot - children make long 'snakes' of clay and wrap them round and round a circular base of clay, to build up the sides of the pot. Use water to smooth the coils together and join the pot.

Support
• Show the children how to stick their thumbs into the ball of clay to make a space for the night light.

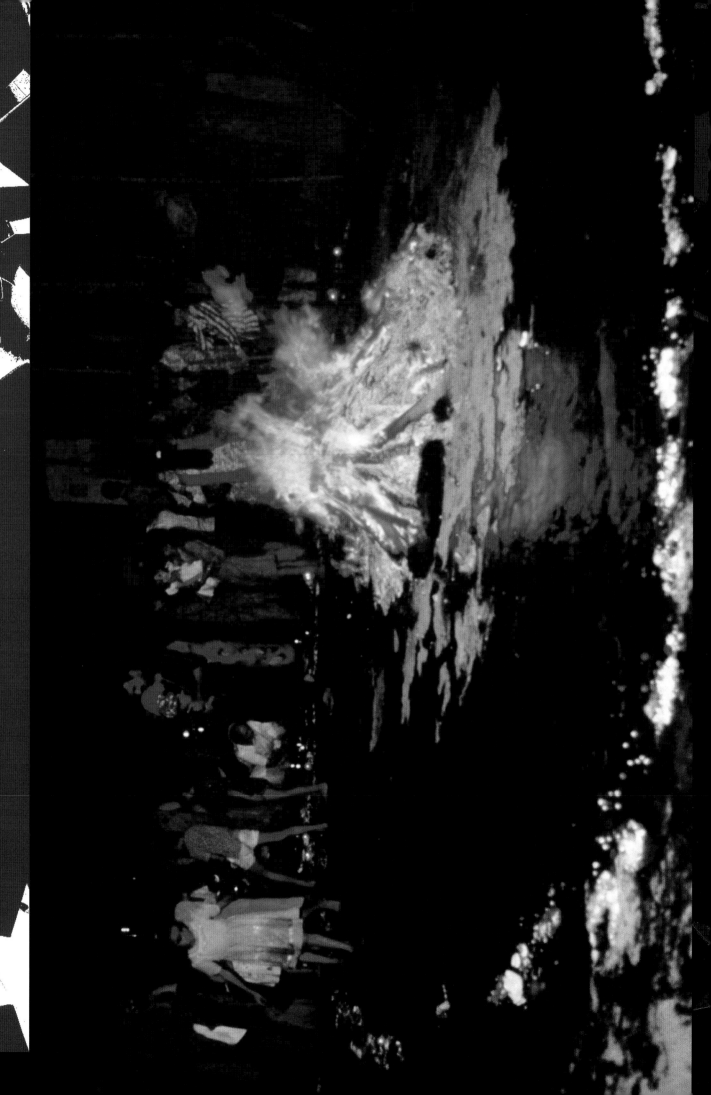

Hinduism: Holi

The Story of Holi

Long ago, there was an evil demon king. He was very rich and powerful, and lived in a magnificent palace. The palace had gleaming white marble walls and golden towers. It had beautiful gardens and flowing fountains, and hundreds of rooms. It had once belonged to Lord Indra, the king of the gods. Until, that is, the wicked demon king threw Lord Indra out of his home.

The demon king was cruel and greedy. He was always shouting and giving orders. Everyone was frightened of him. And woe betide anyone who did not obey his commands. They were harshly punished. For the king thought that he was greater than anyone, even the gods. And he wanted everyone to worship him.

The king had a son called Prahlad. He was not like his father at all. He was very kind and gentle, and worshipped the god Lord Vishnu. One day, the king called for Prahlad.

"My son," he said. "You're a clever boy. Everyone says so. So here's a question for you. Who is the greatest person in the kingdom?"

Prahlad thought for a minute. Then he said, "Father, you are great because you are a king. But Lord Vishnu is greater because he is a god."

The king was furious with his son. His face turned bright red with rage, and he started to splutter and shout.

"How dare you say that to me?" he screamed at Prahlad. "Lord Vishnu, pah! That's not the right answer. I am the greatest in the kingdom. Forget Lord Vishnu, boy. You will worship me!"

"No, father," said Prahlad, quietly. "I will not. I worship Lord Vishnu."

The king was angrier than ever. He decided to give Prahlad a punishment he wouldn't forget. He ordered his soldiers to take Prahlad away and throw him from a cliff.

"That will teach him," he yelled. But Lord Vishnu was watching over Prahlad. Just in time, he saved the boy. Prahlad floated gently down to the ground, as light as a feather.

When the soldiers brought Prahlad safely back to the king, the king exploded with rage.

"Throw him in front of some elephants!" shrieked the king. "See how he likes that!"

So the soldiers took Prahlad and threw him in front of some elephants.

The elephants roared and flapped their ears. They started to charge…straight towards Prahlad. Then suddenly, they stopped and bowed down in front of him. Once again, Lord Vishnu had saved Prahlad.

And once again, the soldiers took Prahlad back to the king. When the soldiers told him what had happened, the king could not believe his ears.

"I don't care how you do it," he screamed at the terrified soldiers. "Just get rid of the boy!"

So the soldiers threw Prahlad into a pit full of poisonous snakes. But the snakes did not bite him. So the soldiers then threw Prahad into a lake. The soldiers tried everything. But nothing could hurt Prahlad. Lord Vishnu was always looking after him.

In a terrible temper, the king went to visit his sister. She was a wicked witch, called Holika.

"You need to show that boy who's in charge," she cackled. "And I've got a brilliant plan to do just that."

And this is what Holika did. She lit a huge bonfire in the palace garden. Soon it was a roaring blaze, with bright, flickering flames leaping up to the sky. Holika called for Prahlad.

"Come on, nephew," she sniggered. "Let's play a game. Hold my hand and walk into the fire with me. Don't worry, dear, you won't get hurt. I've got magic powers, you know. And they will stop us getting burned."

But it was all a trick. Wicked Holika planned to leave Prahlad in the fire. Then she would walk out unharmed.

Holika and Prahlad walked together into the bonfire. Surely, this was the end for Prahlad? But, as so many times before, Lord Vishnu was watching over him. Quick as a flash, he pulled Prahlad out of the flames and Holika died instead.

And to this day, at the festival of Holi, people light blazing bonfires. These remind them of Holika, the wicked witch, who gave Holi its name.

Pictures
Page 58: *On the first night of Holi, people light bonfires to remind them of the story of the wicked witch, Holika. They throw offerings of coconuts and rice into the flames.*
Page 59: *Another Holi custom is to daub each other with coloured powder, water and paint. This is a reminder of a trick played by the god Krishna on his friends, the milkmaids.*

Spraying water

Group of up to 6 children

You will need:
- a large sheet of paper for each child
- felt tip pens
- paintbrushes
- bowls of water
- several different food colourings
- an eye dropper

Explain to the children that during Holi in hot countries, Hindus throw coloured water over each other. This is because the god Krishna is said to have thrown coloured powders over a princess that he loved.

Ask the children what it would be like to have water thrown on them on a cold, British spring day.

Explain that they are going to make pictures of themselves (or each other) so that they can throw water over each other without getting wet.

Get the children to lie flat on a big piece of paper so that you can draw around them one at a time.

When they have got their outline, ask them draw in their features - eyes, nose etc, and to colour some hair.

Pin the finished pictures up outside.

Make the coloured water with the children, using the eye dropper to mix the colours as they wish.

Give each child a bowl of coloured water and a brush and let them flick water over the pictures of their friends.

Extensions
- The child can cut out the outline of themselves.
- The child can colour in the outline with the clothes they are wearing.

Support
- The child can use their hands to flick water over the pictures, rather than a brush.
- If the child doesn't want to lie down to have the outline drawn, draw one for them to colour in.

Early Learning Goal
- Demonstrate fine motor control and co-ordination.

Bonfire collage

Group of up to 10 children

You will need:
- black paper for each child
- tissue paper - orange, yellow, red
- scraps of material - orange, yellow, red
- small twigs
- glue and glue sticks

Explain to the children that one of the reasons Hindus light bonfires is because they believe that fire has the power to clean the land so that the new seeds will grow into good, strong crops.

Give each child a piece of black paper, a glue stick or access to a pot of glue, and let them choose the materials they want to make a picture of a bonfire.

Extensions
- Draw a picture of a bonfire using chalks or pastels.
- Make a model of a bonfire using junk.

Support
- Use glue sticks that are coloured as they go on the paper, but dry clear, so that the children know where they have put the glue.

Early Learning Goal
- Explore colour, shape, texture, form in two dimensions.

Making a 'chir'

Groups of 2/3 children at a time

You will need:
• a long thick stick (8 x 15cm bamboo canes joined together)
• different coloured strips of lightweight cloth
• sticky tape
• scissors

Explain to the whole group of children that a chir is a pole that Hindus put up during Holi. Each strip of cloth is a good luck charm to the Hindus. Explain that everyone is going to make the group's 'chir', but only two or three can work on it at once.

With the small group of children - show them how to pull out the sticky tape, stick one end on the table, and cut a length with their scissors. Get them to choose the cloth they want and stick pieces all down the pole.

At the end of your Holi celebrations, walk around the room with the chir, and some Indian music playing, and let the children each pull off a 'lucky charm' to take home with them.

Extension
• Show the child how to tie longer, heavier strips of cloth on to the pole.

Support
• Use strips of tissue paper to glue onto the pole.

Early Learning Goal
• Handle tools, objects, construction and malleable materials safely and with increasing control.

Full moon biscuits

Group of up to 10 children

You will need:
• a round biscuit for each child
• icing sugar
• water
• hundreds and thousands/sprinkles etc.
• a picture of a full moon
• plastic knives

Explain to the children that the festival of Holi begins when there is a full moon in the sky. Discuss what that means and show them the picture of a full moon.

Let the children each spoon some icing sugar into a bowl. Discuss the texture, feel and smell of it. Ask them how you could change the icing sugar so that you could spread it on the biscuits.

Mix a little water with the icing sugar until it is spreadable.

Give the children each a biscuit and a plastic knife. Let them spread some icing onto their biscuit.

Let the children sprinkle some of the hundreds and thousands onto the icing for decoration.

When you all have full shiny moons, you can say "Holi Hai" - "Holi is here", and eat them!

Early Learning Goals
• Observe, find out about, and identify features in the place they live and the natural world.
• Handle tools safely and with increasing control.

The Story of Wesak

Many, many years ago, a baby was born in a beautiful garden, filled with flowers and fruit trees. It was a clear May night and the moon shone full and round. Angels wrapped the baby in a fine, soft shawl. They showered him with sweet-smelling petals. Then a gentle rumbling earthquake shook the Earth and a bright light shone everywhere. All through the land, there was a feeling of peace and happiness. People forgot their worries and were filled with joy. For this was no ordinary baby.

The baby was named Siddhartha. He was the son of a king. His mother, Queen Maya, took him home to live in the palace. One day, a wise, old man came to visit. He had been travelling for many days. When he saw Siddhartha, his eyes filled with tears.

"Your majesty," he told the king. "Your son will grow up to be a very great man. He may become a king. Or he may become a great holy man, teaching people how to live in peace."

"But why are you crying?" asked the king. "Surely this is good news?"

"I am crying," the old man replied, "because I am very old. I will not live long enough to see it."

The king wanted his son to become a great king and rule the kingdom after him. So he kept him safe inside the palace. Siddhartha had the best of everything – a beautiful palace to live in, fine clothes and fine food. But he often felt unhappy. He thought there must be more to life than this.

One day, Siddhartha left the palace and went for a ride in his chariot. He saw an old man, a sick man and the funeral of a man who had died. Siddhartha was shocked. He had never seen people so unhappy before. Then he saw a holy man, dressed in ragged robes. The holy man had given away everything he owned. But he seemed to be very content with his life.

"I shall be like this holy man," decided Siddhartha. "I shall leave my home and belongings behind."

So that night, in secret, Siddhartha left the palace. He cut off his long, black hair. He changed his fine, silk clothes for simple robes. Then he set off to try to find a way to end all the unhappiness he had seen.

For six long years, Siddhartha lived in the forest with a group of holy men. They lived a very hard life. They ate and drank next to nothing. Soon,

Siddhartha looked like a skeleton. Some days he was so weak he could hardly stand up. But still he did not find the answers he was looking for.

One day, Siddhartha left the forest. He went to a village and sat down, cross-legged, underneath a tall tree.

"I shall stay here," he said, "until I find the truth. However long it takes."

Then he began to meditate. He made his mind become calm and still. All night he sat there, perfectly still and perfectly quiet. And at last, he found the answers he had been looking for. It was like waking up from a long sleep. Now he knew why people suffered and how he could help them find happiness. From then on, he became the Buddha.

The Buddha decided to teach people what he had learned. He gave his first talk in a peaceful deer park.

"People are sad," he said, "because they are never happy with what they have. They always want more."

Then the Buddha taught people a way to stop being unhappy and to find peace. It meant leading a good life, being kind and caring to others, and thinking the right thoughts.

The Buddha spent the rest of his life travelling around India, teaching people how to live. Many people came to hear him and join his followers.

One of them was a terrible robber. But when he heard the Buddha, he gave up his wicked ways.

When the Buddha was about 80 years old, he knew that the time was coming for him to leave the world. His friends did not want him to go.

"Don't be sad," he told them. "I have taught you everything I know. Now I am an old man. When I am gone, carry on my teaching."

The Buddha reached the town of Kushinagara. He stopped to rest in a grove of trees. He lay down on the ground, worn out by the long journey. There he died, as the trees all around him shook and showered him with sweet-smelling petals.

Pictures

Page 64: *A Buddhist kneels before an image of the Buddha in the vihara. At Wesak, a special puja is held at which people pay their respects to the Buddha.*

Page 65: *A girl holds some flowers to offer to the Buddha at Wesak. Flowers are important symbols in Buddhism. They look lovely but soon fade and die, reminding people of the Buddha's teaching that nothing lasts for ever.*

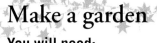

Make a garden

You will need:
• a shallow cardboard tray for each child (or thick card about the size of an ice cream tub lid)
• twigs - enough for one for each child
• pink, yellow, and orange tissue paper
• brown modelling clay
• green paint mixed with PVA glue
• a paintbrush for each child
• glue sticks

Read the story to the children and explain that they are going to make a garden like the one that Siddhartha was born in.

Get the children to paint the card or cardboard tray with the green paint and PVA. Leave to dry.

Give the children a twig each and a lump of modelling clay. Show them how to make the modelling clay into a mound and push the twig into it so that it doesn't fall over.

Now they can decorate the twig with some blossom.

Ask the children to tear off bits of pink tissue paper, crumple them gently and stick onto the twigs to make blossom trees for the garden.

When the green paint is dry, push the brown modelling clay with the blossom tree onto the tray.

If the children want to, they can make flowers for the garden with different coloured tissue paper crumpled and stuck onto the 'grass'.

Extension
• The children could make a little baby out of the modelling clay to lie in the garden.

A lotus flower

Group of up to 6 children

You will need:
• a paper plate for each child
• coloured card cut into petal shapes so that 8 of these shapes fit around the paper plate
• picture of a lotus flower (water lily)
• PVA glue
• glue sticks
• paint and brushes

Show the children the picture of the lotus flower. Explain that the lotus is important to Buddhists because it tells them that everyone can grow and reach enlightenment, just as a lotus grows through the waters of a pond to reach the light.

Give each child a paper plate and ask them to count out 8 petals.

They stick the petals round the edge of the plate. Then they can paint the middle of the plate.

Extension
• Number the petals 1 - 8 so that the children need to find one of each number.

Support
• Mix PVA in with the paint and get the children to paint the plate first and then stick the petals directly onto the gluey paint.

Early Learning Goal
Count reliably up to 10 everyday objects.

Wesak candles

Groups of up to 6 children

You will need:
• strips of coloured beeswax (about 10 x 5cm)
• modelling clay
• lids of jars
• scissors
• candle wick

Explain to the children that Buddhists carry candles at Wesak to show that the Buddha's wisdom lights up the darkness of ignorance.

Let each child choose a strip of wax. Help them measure and cut a length of wick that is a few centimetres longer than the width of wax.

Show the children how to roll the wax around the wick, and then to keep rolling it around until they have made a small candle.

Get the children to place their candle on a jar lid, and then to decorate the lid with flowers/shapes made out of the playdough.

N.B. Make sure the children understand that they must ask an adult to light the candle. Have a discussion about the danger of matches.

Extension
• Ask the children to measure the width of the wax with a ruler and cut a piece of wick longer than their measurement.
• Explain that the number eight is important to Buddhists because the Buddha taught eight important ways to live, called the Noble Eightfold Path.

Support
• The adult rolls the wick around the wax to start it off, then the child finishes rolling.

Early Learning Goal
• Demonstrate fine motor control and co-ordination.

The wheel of life

Group of up to 10 children

You will need:
• a large card circle for each child
• variety of circles smaller than the main circle
• circles or milk bottle lids, lids of jars etc.
• PVA glue
• glue sticks

Explain that the Buddha said that life was like a wheel. Ask the children what shape a wheel is. Can they find anything else that is the same shape? Tell them they are going to make a wheel collage.

Give each child a large circle and let them choose from all the other circular items the ones they want to stick on their wheel of life.

Extensions
• Explain that the wheel of life meant birth, death and rebirth - that Buddhists believe after we die we are born again in a different body.
• Ask the child how many wheels they have put on their big wheel.

Early Learning Goal
• Use language such as 'circle' or 'bigger' to describe the shape and size of solids and flat shapes.

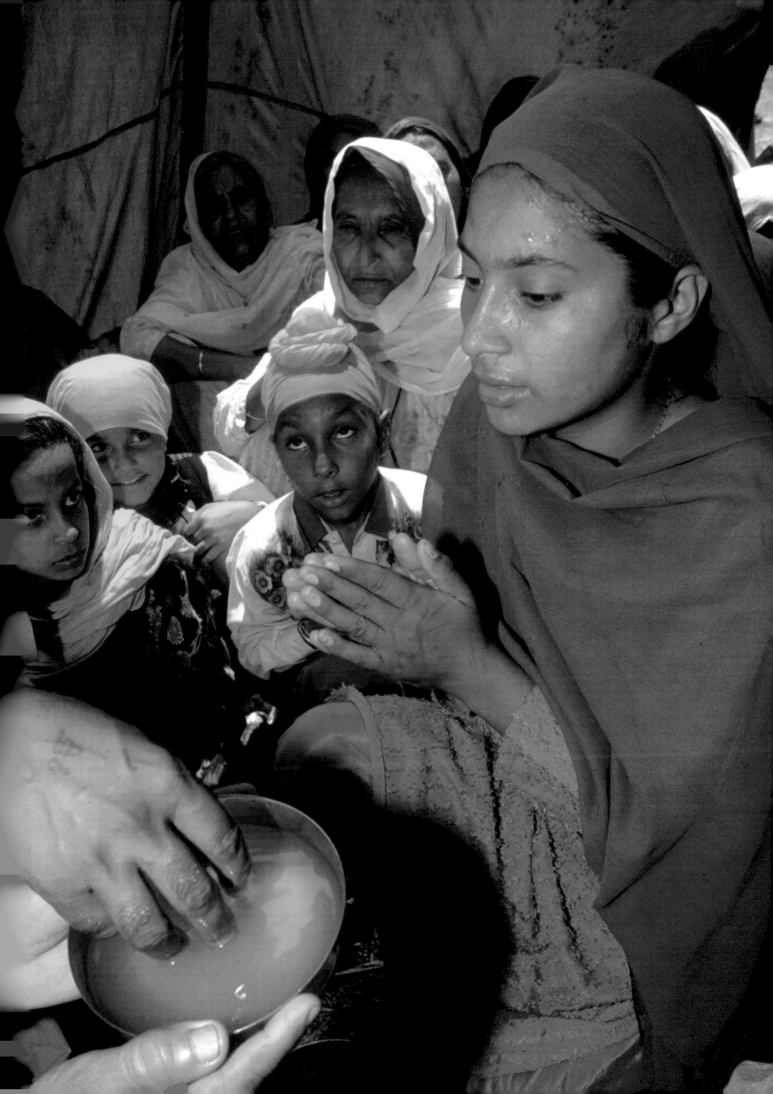

The Story of Baisakhi

The tenth great teacher of the Sikhs was called Guru Gobind Singh. There are many stories about him. One spring day, hundreds of years ago, Guru Gobind Singh called all the Sikhs together. He told them to come to the town of Anandapur where he lived. Thousands of Sikhs came from all over India to the town. This was a special time of year when Sikhs celebrated the festival of Baisakhi. They always looked forward to it very much. But this year, they were even more excited than usual. The Guru himself had called them to Anandapur. Surely, this meant something extra special was about to happen?

A huge crowd of Sikhs gathered. Guru Gobind Singh stood in front of them. He was wearing a bright yellow turban on his head, and bright yellow robes with a blue sash. In his hand, he held a long, gleaming sword. For many years, the Sikhs had been badly treated because of their religion. Now Guru Gobind Singh wanted them to stand up for what they believed in. He wanted to find out how brave and strong they really were. That is why he had called them together.

"It is time for all of you to be brave," Guru Gobind Singh told the Sikhs, holding up his sword. "Now, which one of you is ready to die for your faith?"

The crowd went silent. Nobody moved or spoke. They were all very frightened by the Guru's words. None of them knew what he meant. And none of them wanted to die.

So the Guru asked his question a second time.

"Who is ready to die for their faith?" he said. "Are any of you brave enough?"

Still nobody answered. The Guru asked his question a third time.

"I am asking you again," he said. "Are any of you ready to die for your faith?"

This time, a man stepped forward. He walked bravely through the crowd towards the Guru.

"My name is Darya Ram," he said. "I am ready to give up my life for God."

Guru Gobind Singh led Darya Ram into his tent. A few minutes later, the Guru came out again. His sword was stained red with blood. The crowd gasped in horror. Some people started to leave. But many others stayed behind. They wanted to know what would happen next.

Once again, the Guru asked his question. "Who here is ready to die for their faith?"

Another man stepped forward and the Guru led him into the tent. Then the Guru came out again, his sword covered in blood.

The Guru asked his question three more times. And three more men stepped forward. One by one, the Guru led them into his tent. Soon five brave men had gone inside. The crowd was very sad. They thought all the five men had been killed.

Then an amazing thing happened. Guru Gobind Singh came out of the tent, leading all five of the men. The men were all alive! People could not believe their eyes. What was going on?

The men were wearing bright yellow turbans on their heads, and bright yellow robes, with blue sashes. Just like Guru Gobind Singh. And each of them carried a long, gleaming sword. Just like Guru Gobind Singh.

"These men have shown how brave they are," Guru Gobind Singh told the crowd. "They were all ready to die for their faith. They have been chosen by God. From now on, they will be called the Five Beloved Ones."

Then Guru Gobind Singh mixed some sugar and water together in a bowl. He gave it to the Five Beloved Ones to drink. Then he took a drink from the same bowl. This showed that everyone was equal in God's eyes. After that, many more Sikhs came forward to join the Five Beloved Ones.

Pictures
Page 70: *At Baisakhi, special services are held in the Gurdwara. The Harimandir, or Golden Temple, in Amritsar, India, is the Sikhs' holiest Gurdwara.*
Page 71: *A Sikh girl joining the Khalsa at a special amrit ceremony held at Baisakhi. This is a reminder of what happened at the first Baisakhi.*

Five beans

Groups of 2,4 or 6 children

You will need:
• enough beans so that every pair of children has five
• number cards 1-5

Explain to the children that the number five is important to Sikhs, because there were five men who were willing to give up their lives for God when the Guru asked them at Baisakhi.

Put the children into pairs and ask each pair to take 5 beans. One child takes some of his beans and hides them in his hands.

The other child guesses how many beans the other child is holding and then says, "Show me the beans please."

The child with the beans lets the other child count how many beans s/he has and then find the number card to match the number of beans.

The children take it in turns to hide and count.

Extension
• The child guessing says whether there is an odd or even number in the hands.
• Write the number of beans on a piece of paper.

Support
• Number cards have dots as well as the number.
• Reduce the number of beans.

Early Learning Goal
• Recognise numerals 1-5.

Make a flower garland

Group of up to 6 children

You will need:
• long ribbons/strips of card (about 30 x 5cm)
• green tissue paper
• tissue paper - different colours
• glue sticks

Explain to the children that during the festival of Baisakhi the Sikhs hang garlands of flowers on their doors.

Give each child a ribbon or strip of card, and let them tear up squares of green tissue paper to stick all the way down the strip. Then bring out the coloured tissue and let the children tear pieces off, crumple them up and stick onto the green squares to produce a flower garland. Hang the garlands round the room and on the door.

Support
• Use just coloured tissue and leave out the green squares.

Early Learning Goal
• Explore colour, texture, shape, form and space in two dimensions.

Make banana cake

Group of up to 6 children

You will need
• a large mixing bowl
• a fork or potato masher
• a sieve
• 3 bananas
• 1 cup milk
• 1 cup flour
• 1 cup sugar
• half-teaspoon baking powder
• half-teaspoon ground cardamon
• a bread tin

Tell the children that Sikhs have special things to eat at Baisakhi because it is a special festival to them. One of these things can be banana cake.

Adult set the oven temperature to 350°F/ 180°C/ gas mark 4.

Help the children to measure out the cups of milk, sugar and flour.

Get the children to peel the bananas and mash with the milk and sugar.

Help the children sieve the flour, cardamon and baking powder and mix into the banana mixture. Put the mixture into a greased bread tin.

All the time, encourage the children to talk about the ingredients using their senses. Discuss the smell of the cardamon, the look of the mixtures, and introduce new vocabulary such as mushy, powdery, stiff, etc.

Encourage the children to discuss what changes will take place during cooking. Will the cake come out of the oven looking the same as it went in?

Bake the cake for 40 minutes, or until the cake comes away from the sides of the tin. The cake is of a moist consistency.

Early Learning Goals
• Look closely at similarities, differences, patterns and change.
• Investigate objects and materials by using their senses as appropriate.

Music and dance
Whole group activity

You will need
• Four different musical instruments, for example a drum, a tambourine, agogo and chime bars

Tell the children that the festival of Baisakhi celebrates the harvest. Many Sikhs celebrate with music and dance to say thank you to God for giving them food. These dances show how the land is ploughed, the seeds sown, the weeds pulled and then the crop harvested.

Discuss how you could dance to show the ploughing of the land and which instrument would be best for this action.

Go through all four activities, helping the children to develop actions for ploughing, sowing, weeding and harvesting.

Play the instruments in turn and encourage the children to put the action to the instrument.

Let the children take turns to play the instruments and decide when to change.

Extensions
• Make up a story with the children about a farmer.
• Use just a drum, but different beats to show the different activities.

Support
• Use a tape or CD of Indian music and let the children do their own actions for the farming activities.

Early Learning Goal
• Express and communicate their ideas by using a variety of musical instruments.

Christian calendar

6 January	Epiphany
7 January	Christmas Day (Orthodox Church)
March/April	Easter
April/May	Ascension Day
May/June	Pentecost
September/October	Harvest Festival
November/December	Advent Sunday
25 December	Christmas Day

Hindu calendar

February/March	Mahashivaratri
February/March	Holi
March/April	Ramanavami
July/August	Raksha Bandhan
August/September	Janmashtami
September/October	Durga Puja
September/October	Dassehra
October/November	Divali

Jewish calendar

February/March	Purim
March/April	Pesach
May/June	Shavuot
September/October	Rosh Hashanah
September/October	Yom Kippur
September/October	Sukkot
September/October	Simchat Torah
November/December	Hanukkah

Buddhist calendar

February	Losar
April	Hana-Matsuri
April/May	Wesak
June/July	Poson
July/August	O-bon
July/August	Asala
October/November	Kathina
November	Sangha Day

Islamic calendar

Muharram	Al-Hijrah
Muharram	Ashura
Rabi' al-Awwal	Milad al-Nabi
Rajab	Laylat-ul-Isra
Ramadan	Ramadan
Ramadan	Laylat-ul-Qadr
Shawwal	Id-ul-Fitr
Dhul-Hijjah	Id-ul-Adha

Note: These are the months of the Islamic lunar calendar which has a shorter year than the Western calendar. Muslim festivals, therefore, fall at different times each year.

Sikh calendar

February/March	Hola Mohalla
April	Baisakhi
June	Guru Arjun Dev's martyrdom
October/November	Divali
October/November	Guru Nanak's birthday
November/December	Guru Tegh Bahadur's martyrdom
December/January	Guru Gobind Singh's birthday

Glossary

Akhand Path A continuous reading of the Guru Granth Sahib from beginning to end.

Allah The Islamic word for God in the Arabic language.

Amrit Water sweetened with sugar used in ceremonies initiating Sikhs into the Khalsa.

Baptised When a person becomes a member of the Christian Church, at a ceremony involving being sprinkled with or immersed in water.

Bible The Christian scriptures, consisting of the Old and the New Testaments.

Brahman The great spirit or soul in Hinduism. Everything comes from Brahman and Brahman is everywhere. Some Hindus call Brahman God.

Carols Christian songs sung at Christmas.

Church (Lower case 'c') A Christian place of worship. (Upper case 'C') The whole Christian community or a particular Christian denomination.

Covenant In Judaism, an agreement made between God and Abraham. Abraham and his descendants (the Jews) would worship only God. Then God would watch over them and lead them to the Promised Land (of Israel).

Crucifixion A method of executing criminals in Roman times. The culprit was tied or nailed to a cross and left to die. This is how Jesus Christ was put to death.

Dreidel A spinning top used to play a traditional game at the Jewish festival of Hanukkah.

Enlightenment An experience of seeing and realising the truth. The word is particularly associated with Buddhism.

Eucharist A Christian ceremony which remembers the life and death of Jesus Christ through the sharing of blessed bread and wine. Also called Mass; Holy Communion.

Exodus The liberation of the Jews from slavery in Egypt.

Gurdwara A Sikh place of worship. The word literally means 'the gateway to the Guru'. Any place that contains a copy of the Guru Granth Sahib can be called a Gurdwara.

Gurpurbs Sikh festivals marking events in the Gurus' lives, such as the anniversaries of their births or deaths.

Guru The title given to the ten holy teachers of Sikhism and to the Guru Granth Sahib.

Guru Granth Sahib The name of the Sikh scriptures.

Haggadah A book used at the Seder supper to tell the story of the Jewish festival of Pesach. The word 'Haggadah' means 'the telling'.

Hametz Any food made with yeast or leavened dough. This is 'forbidden' food and must be removed from homes before the Jewish festival of Pesach.

Hanukiah A nine-branched candlestick lit at the Jewish festival of Hanukkah.

Ihram The plain, white clothes worn by male Muslim pilgrims on the Hajj to Makkah to show the equality and purity of the pilgrims. Women wear their usual, modest dress.

Jesus Christ The central figure of Christianity, believed by Christians to be the son of God.

Karma In Hinduism and Buddhism, the law of cause and effect. Good actions in this life lead to a higher rebirth; bad actions lead to a lower rebirth.

Khalsa The Sikh community.

Madinah The city in Saudi Arabia to which the Prophet Muhammad migrated in 622 CE and where he established the first Muslim community.

Makkah The city in Saudi Arabia in which the Prophet Muhammad was born and the focus of the Hajj pilgrimage.

Mandir A Hindu place of worship. Also called a temple.

Matzah A flat, cracker-like type of Jewish bread made from dough which has not been allowed to rise. Plural: matzot.

Moksha Ultimate liberation from the continuous cycle of birth, death and rebirth.

Moses The Jewish leader chosen by God to lead the Jews out of Egypt and to receive God's revelation of the Torah on Mt Sinai.

Mosque A Muslim place of the worship. The Arabic word is masjid.

Muhammad The name of the last and greatest prophet of Islam. The names of the prophets are often followed by the letters 'pbuh' meanings 'peace and blessings upon him'.

Murti A sacred image or picture of a Hindu deity which is used as the focus for worship. Calling a murti a statue may cause offence.

Nirvana In Buddhism, a state of perfect peace that follows when people overcome greed, hatred and ignorance and become free from the cycle of birth, death and rebirth.

Paschal Relating to the Christian festival of Easter.

Puja In Hinduism, the way in which Hindus worship. In Buddhism, the way in which Buddhist honour the Buddha (many Buddhists do not like the word worship).

Qur'an The sacred book of Islam which was revealed to the Prophet Muhammad and contains Allah's wishes for the world.

Rabbi A Jewish teacher and leader of the Jewish community.

Resurrection The rising from the dead of Jesus Christ on the third day after his crucifixion. A fundamental tenet of Christianity as the basis of a new, or risen, life for all Christians.

Revelation The communication of the Qur'an from Allah to the Prophet Muhammad.

Sanatana dharma Eternal teaching. The name Hindus give to their religious beliefs.

Seder The name of the meal eaten at the Jewish festival of Pesach and of the plate containing various symbolic foods.

Shabads Sikh sacred hymns from the Guru Granth Sahib which are sung at services in the Gurdwara.

Shabbat The Jewish day of rest and prayer which begins at sunset on Friday and lasts until nightfall on Saturday. Also called Sabbath.

Synagogue A Jewish place of worship.

Tenakh The 24 books of the Hebrew (Jewish) Bible, including the Torah, Nevi'im and Ketuvim.

Ten Commandments Ten laws which Jews and Christians use as guides for how God wishes them to lead their lives. Also called the Ten Sayings.

Torah The five books of teaching which form the most important part of the Jewish scriptures.

Vihara In Buddhism, a temple or monastery (often the two are combined).

Note for Teachers

Early learning goals for all activities in the book:

PSE
• Have a developing respect for their own cultures and beliefs and those of other people.
• Understand that people have different cultures and beliefs that need to be treated with respect.
• Understand that they can expect others to treat their cultures and beliefs with respect.
• Work as part of a group or class.

Knowledge and Understanding of the World
• Begin to know about their own cultures and beliefs and those of other people.

For this activity:
• Work as part of a group taking turns, understanding that there need to be agreed values and codes of behaviour for groups of people, adults and children alike, to work together.
• Sustain attentive listening, responding to what they have heard with relevant comments, questions or actions.
• Extend their vocabulary, exploring meanings and sounds of new words.
• Re-tell narratives in the correct sequence, drawing on language patterns of stories.

Home links for all festivals
• Put a letter out to parents explaining which festival you will be learning about, and asking if they can send in any instruments, clothing, or relevant items for the children to see.
• Invite in people who follow the religion you are studying to show the children specific things about the festival - e.g how to put on a sari during Divali etc., how to cook specific food for the festival etc.

Index